FREEDOM FROM FEAR MEANS CONFIDENCE AND COURAGE—HEALTH AND HAPPINESS.

Fear is real. It darkens lives, stalls careers, ruins relationships. Although the anxieties we may have of public speaking, driving, swimming—or of fear itself—are irrational, even imaginary, their crippling effects are all too real.

Fear can strike anyone. Salespeople become afraid to call on clients. Housewives tremble at the thought of a bridge party. Football players lose their nerve. Executives hide behind their secretaries. Celebrities get stage fright.

It happens all the time. *But fear can be conquered.* No one has to remain a hostage to their phobias. *Help is here.*

FEAR NO MORE

Author Diane F. Hailparn earned her M.S. at Columbia University. Her practice includes the supervision of other therapists, and her step-by-step techniques have helped thousands overcome their anxieties and fear. *Now you can overcome yours!*

FEAR NO MORE

A
PSYCHOTHERAPIST'S
GUIDE FOR
OVERCOMING YOUR
ANXIETIES
AND PHOBIAS

DIANE F. HAILPARN M.A., M.S.

SMP

ST. MARTIN'S PAPERBACKS

FEAR NO MORE: A PSYCHOTHERAPIST'S GUIDE FOR OVERCOMING YOUR ANXIETIES AND PHOBIAS

Copyright © 1988 by Diane F. Hailparn

Library of Congress Catalog Card Number 88-39969

ISBN: 0-312-92328-7

Printed in the United States of America

St. Martin's Press hardcover edition published 1988
St. Martin's Paperbacks edition/October 1990

10 9 8 7 6 5 4 3 2 1

To Michael, as always, with love, affection, and admiration.

CONTENTS

ACKNOWLEDGMENTS

Special thanks goes to my editor, Tom Dunne, for his belief in this material. His insights into the book's direction were very valuable to me, and very much appreciated. And to his editorial assistant, David Hirshfeld, who answered my questions with energy and enthusiasm; for his support I thank him.

My gratitude goes out to Dr. George Weinberg, whose talents are a constant source of inspiration. His encouragement in the project has been very special indeed.

An important note of appreciation is due to Helen McDermott, whose insights and vitality assisted me in countless ways. Her warm support is greatly valued.

In addition, I would like to mention those colleagues whose reactions I found so helpful—Drs. David Balderston, John Crandall, Lucinda Mermin, and Phil Roskam.

I have been fortunate over the years to have accompanied many of my patients on their journey of self-discovery as they reached new levels of awareness, success, and happiness. I thank them for inviting me on such an important quest.

And thanks to my European friends, whose *joie de vivre* touches me in countless ways, while replenishing the mind and spirit.

And to my husband, Michael, whose love, respect, and encouragement provided an infinite source of strength to me. His warmth and generosity is a gift I treasure dearly.

INTRODUCTION

I believe that anyone can conquer fear by doing the things they fear to do, provided they keep doing them until they get a record of successful experiences behind them.

—Eleanor Roosevelt

THIS book is written for anyone who suffers from irrational fears in any form —those emotions that hold you back from becoming all you can be. Your anxieties may severely limit your functioning or may be only a minor inconvenience. They may embarrass you in public, or hurt you only in private. Either way, you may consciously know that it makes no rational sense whatsoever to feel as you do. Yet reason and rationality don't seem to apply, or even to help, when you're face to face with your fears.

But now you're going to change all that. Step by step you will learn to cope with, understand, and overcome your fears, anxieties, and phobias. The journey is going to be rough at times and cause you moments of doubt, yet the rewards you reap will far outweigh the stress you feel. Change is never easy. It requires discipline, commitment to yourself, and risks. But a life free from crippling fear is well worth all that, and more.

The purpose of this book is to show you how to deal with such anxious feelings, first to *identify* them, then to begin to *understand* how and why they work, and finally to move toward *conquering* them. I'm not suggesting it's going to be easy. A lot depends on you and how much effort you're willing to exert and motivation you feel. Be aware that sometimes it's going to feel like a lonely, frustrating struggle, with setbacks along the way. But the rewards are enormous and can change your life. Even before the journey is completed, there will be many small moments of triumph that help to guide you and give you hope. What we have to do together is to help you conquer these imaginary tigers that growl at you in restaurants, haunt the elevators, and enter the car with you. Slowly you are going to confront your fears so that you can start to have a new life free from all this anxiety. The key to remember is small steps are better than no steps at all. So what if all you can do today is get behind the wheel of the car? You don't have to drive at this point in time. But try not to see the car as a mocking reminder of what you can't do. Instead, begin to see it as a challenge of what's ahead. One thing is sure: you've taken the first steps by picking up this book and reading this far! That says something about you and your desire to move ahead.

People want to believe that there's an instant cure to every problem. Our society is full of come-on advertisements for products that claim to satisfy your every need. Rejuvenating cosmetics and face lifts offer quickie solutions to aging. They all promise a new you. This "quick-fix" attitude is a belief in what one psychologist calls "The Pill Fairy." Just one swallow and all is different.

But relief can almost never be achieved without effort. Success and achievement come through hard work and, most important, belief in yourself. It probably has been a while since you've believed in you. Now it's time to begin a program that helps you to love and accept yourself, with all your strengths and weaknesses.

Your very efforts here are crucial to success. The end result is a commitment toward a life without the constraints of fears, anxieties, and phobias. Instead, you'll develop an ability to move ahead and start enjoying situations and people without dreading a fear attack.

Fortunately, you won't be taking the trip alone. Not only will I be there with you, helping to chart the direction, but millions of other sufferers are rooting for you. These people have won their battles and would readily understand the struggle that's ahead. If they knew you, they would be sympathetic with your endeavors and rejoice in your successes.

Together we are going to explore alternative ways of thinking about your fears, so that you can break out of the negative pattern you're now in. You will begin to move forward and overcome your fears, anxieties, and phobias, in whatever form they take or whatever arena they're played out in. The time has come to stop allowing these ideas to rule your life. You are a victim of your own imagination. Instead of envisioning catastrophic scenarios, you are going to use your talents to imagine a more realistic and happier future.

The general plan of this book is first to examine what your fears are, how they began and took shape, and what you can do to overcome them. It's important to demystify your fears so that they become understandable and more concrete to you. Far too often the anxiety you feel overwhelms you and takes on a power that rules your life. It might be the fear of public speaking, flying, or stepping into that ominous shopping mall. Whatever your particular fear, anxiety, or phobia, it restricts rather than expands your opportunities.

For the moment, imagine yourself without all those catastrophic thoughts that you carry around daily! Entering a museum without worrying about dizziness, or boarding a bus without feeling trapped. Accepting a date without all the troublesome expectations, or just learning how to make casual connections with people without anxiety. This is precisely my ultimate goal for you.

By following the principles outlined in the book and giving yourself time to work with them, you can begin your new life, free from the tight reins of a phobia or overwhelming fear. No longer will those anxious thoughts bounce around in your head, creating doubts.

So prepare yourself for what could be the most important journey you've ever taken. Perseverance will be rewarded and all it takes is your determination and willingness to try. Together we will embark on this exciting and rewarding adventure that will open up new horizons for you. I'll be illuminating the way for you so that you'll be able to see more clearly your path to success.

PART ONE

UNDERSTANDING YOUR FEARS

IN this part of the book, I want to introduce you to what fears and phobias are.

Many people don't really understand what their anxieties are all about, or why they were "selected" to be more fearful than the next person. I want to give you such knowledge so that you will become aware of what your fears are, and how they limit you.

Individually, you may have such fears as driving, giving a talk before a group, standing in line in a store, heights, flying, elevators, or perhaps just fearing the feelings themselves. An underlying dynamic could be a deep anxiety about success so that you have subtle (or not so subtle) ways of defeating yourself.

Whatever your fears are, I want you to begin to get an insight into what you are experiencing, so that you can realize how and why your anxiety occurs. In other words, I want you to become an expert on yourself, so that you'll start to gain control over your fears, rather than having them control you. This is the first step toward fearing no more.

CHAPTER ONE

WHY ME?

WHY me?

You've probably asked yourself this question a thousand times. "Why is it that everyone else steps on a plane, asks for their favorite magazine, and then casually reads it? Meanwhile I'm in agony wondering if my life is about to end. I panic the second I hear that announcement to fasten my seat belt."

Fearful people are always asking themselves why destiny selected them to carry such torturous anxiety. Other people seem to breeze through the same situation without panic. They step into elevators without a care in the world. Shopping and driving doesn't faze them. Their hearts don't start pounding at the sight of a dog being walked nearby. Every morning they leave their houses and cross the street to have coffee with a neighbor as if it were nothing. Why me? You have every right to ask such a question! It certainly is unfair that some people are more susceptible to painful, anxious feelings, whereas others aren't.

Research on phobias and fears in general suggests at least some reasons why particular people fall prey to them and others don't. In recent years we've been able to identify certain traits that many anxious people have in common. Not only that, but certain early influences that predispose one to suffer in this way have been identified.

Fearful people include artists, writers, musicians, and other talented people who are quite successful in relationships with both family and friends. Many anxious people are successful businesspeople and pillars of their community. Yet what all of them have in common is fear, anxiety, and self-doubt.

Unfortunately many people constrict themselves with their fears so that they don't realize their potential and talents. "If only I weren't so anxious I'd audition for the part." "I'd love to fly to Europe, but the thought of flying terrifies me." "I want that promotion, but it means taking the elevator to the sixtieth floor every day. But I can't, so forget it."

Think about some of the traits that many fearful people have in common.

1. Fearful people usually tend to be very *sensitive* and overly aware of other people's reactions.
2. They are highly *imaginative*. Often their thinking takes place in the form of mental pictures.

3. They are *negative* thinkers in their feared situations, concerned about the worst that can possibly happen to them.
4. Many have a feeling of *insecurity* and have lost confidence in themselves.
5. They tend to give an *outwardly calm* appearance while churning inside.
6. They want to *please*. They tend to do what others want rather than please themselves.
7. They are *self-conscious*, easily embarrassed, and overly concerned about what other people think of them.
8. They tend to be placid and fit into their environment, avoiding conflicts and even hiding from them.[1]

So why were you "selected" to be fearful? Glancing at the above list you see that it includes many positive qualities—sensitivity, creativity, and a desire to please others. The problem is that you take the ball and run with it! Not only are you aware of others, but, alas, a bit *too* concerned with what they may think and say about you.

Bob, a salesman for a major retail clothing manufacturer, felt extremely anxious whenever he had to do sales presentations. He dreaded them with a passion. The mere thought of standing up before his co-workers was enough to make him break out into a cold sweat. Bob would imagine that his mind would go blank and that he'd look like a fool, not to mention becoming the laughingstock of the whole company.

He constantly obsessed to his wife, Donna, about the

other people and how "cool, calm, and collected they looked." Meanwhile he saw himself as a shrivelling bundle of nerves. He tortured himself with constant "Why me?" thoughts. "All the others can get up and do these stupid presentations without blinking an eye. I'm the only one who dreads those damn meetings!"

What Bob failed to realize is that most people are anxious, but that his imagination had a grip on him that he felt was unshakable. He mistakenly idealized his co-workers' calm exteriors as an indicator of how they felt inside. This made him feel lonely and isolated. He believed that he had this horrible secret (his anxiety) that if discovered would render him vulnerable, and possibly cost him his job. Bob's imagination let him see only the worst that could happen. He engaged in what is called "catastrophic thinking," leaving him no room for a positive outcome.

In reality, as I later found out, some of Bob's co-workers were so out of touch with people's feelings in general they wouldn't have known what a vulnerable person looked like. They concealed their feelings with grandiosity. Others didn't suffer at work, but had different problems, particularly in relationships; they didn't have real friends or love anyone. Thus they appeared confident and carefree because they invested nothing in other people.

Often we feel we're the only ones who are afraid of our own shadow. Yet as human beings we are prone to continual levels of anxiety. There are plenty of things for a creative mind to seize upon. Just pick up a newspaper, watch television, even talk to a neighbor, and you are almost sure to hear about illness, divorce, violence, or dozens of other crises. We are constantly being reminded of our own frailties and how little control we actually have over our lives. What is special about us is that we translate this information into morbid and catastrophic fears.

It is especially important for you to know that anxiety is part of life. Everyone feels anxious. What matters is how the feeling manifests itself. It becomes a problem when the intensity is overwhelming and fear develops, giving you the feeling that you must be crazy. The man next to you in the restaurant eating alone seems to be enjoying himself, chatting with the waiter, reading a newspaper. Meanwhile you're sitting in an agitated state, squirming in your seat. Or the women driving her car up to the toll booth at the ominous bridge looks calm, while you wonder how in God's name you'll manage to cross that bridge without meeting your fate.

Again, you ask yourself "Why me?" as if some special force singled you out. But remember that you really are not alone in your struggle to overcome your fears. There are millions of fearful and anxious people out there who feel as you do. But there are an awful lot of people who don't have to face their fears and admit to them as you might. People who live in cities where public transportation is readily available don't have to confront the fear of driving. If they're afraid of getting on a plane, then they can take a train (time permitting). If they fear speaking out in public, but are sitting in the audience, then they're just fine at the same meeting where Bob was in a panic. Of course if these same people move to the suburbs and are forced to drive a car, or as part of the business are required to fly, there's no more avoidance!

John had a terror of flying, yet his wife Susan couldn't

understand why he made such a fuss. Although she listened sympathetically, she often told him to "just get on the plane and forget about it." Then John took a new job in New York City with a major insurance company. He and Susan moved into an apartment on the upper west side of Manhattan.

One day, after a particularly stressful week, Susan was riding the subway home from the Wall Street firm she worked at. Suddenly she felt extremely anxious. Her throat began to close and she trembled. She prayed for the train to get to the next station. Her heart pounded so fiercely she thought she might be having a heart attack. Each second seemed like an eternity. Susan staggered off the train and somehow made it through the exit doors and up the stairs to the sunlight. Only then did the symptoms pass. When she described her ordeal to John, he knew immediately what had happened, since this was exactly how he felt when boarding a plane.

This is not an unusual story. Perhaps it is not as consoling as it could be, right now, to know that you are not alone, that the fear you carry around is shared by others.

You may be thinking, "But I feel it now! I feel alone and crazy today." Yet while you may feel crazy, you're not crazy! It's just that your fears are immediate and very present (not to mention painful). But they don't have to continue. That's what this book is all about, to help you identify your fears, realize that you are not alone, and move past these scary thoughts and start living life free from fears and phobias.

Let's study more closely some of the qualities that sufferers have in common. I have already suggested imagination—the ability to see things that could exist. Imagination is a wonderful trait . . . except when you turn it against yourself. You could use it to envision a successful business meeting, finish a novel, give a super performance, and deal sensitively with your children. These are all life-enhancing experiences. You can use imagination in the service of positive thinking and to make you feel alive and rejuvenated. Or you can allow your imagination to take hold of you in a negative way and leave you very scared.

You think negative thoughts and then picture them in your mind's eye as disastrous, catastrophic, and demeaning. Anticipatory anxiety grips you and makes you feel threatened and terribly afraid. You see yourself as a trembling, speechless wreck. Or you see the papers you hold trembling and people wondering what that rustling on the stage is. Think of yourself as not merely beset by imagination, but as misusing it. Right now you are using your imagination as a torturous weapon against yourself. Instead of picturing success you see failure and humiliation. Thus you feel discouraged and drained.

Many anxious people have admirable traits. They are known for being competent workers and excellent spouses. They are loyal and committed to relationships. But one of the problems underlying their fears and anxieties is that these people often sacrifice their needs and wishes just to please others and gain their approval.

Joan, an attractive, soft-spoken woman in her mid-thirties, worked as an art director for an advertising firm in San Francisco. She was well respected by her colleagues and liked by her friends. But Joan suffered from a powerful fear: she dreaded asserting herself. Her char-

9

acter fit the pattern of many fearful people. She had imagination, intelligence, and an eagerness to please and do a good job. But she avoided any confrontation with people, especially at work. Nor could she assert herself with friends, even when they deserved a confrontation. She imagined she'd be rejected or laughed at behind her back. Her imagination provided all kinds of humiliation scenarios.

Thus people took advantage of her. She had a tendency to pick up the check at lunch or dinner, and often the gesture was not reciprocated. At work, she couldn't bring herself to ask her secretary to stay after five o'clock, even a few extra minutes—despite the fact that the secretary often took an hour and a half for lunch! To make matters worse, Joan inconvenienced herself by staying late to finish the work her secretary was responsible for.

This desire to be liked interfered continually with her ability to connect with her own needs and wants. Although Joan would agree to do things, she actually resented the request, but didn't say anything. She would do the same thing when faced with an unpleasant situation: avoid rather than confront. Instead of admitting that she felt victimized at times by her secretary and friends, she was only able to feel "victimized" by her fears. "I hate being this way!" she lamented. "It exposes me as being so vulnerable. How in God's name did I ever get this way?"

As you become more acquainted with other fears in this book, perhaps the endless search for the "Why me?" answers will be more understandable. Also, as you begin to know yourself more, you will develop a real appreciation for your sensitivity and aliveness. Now it's time to begin to cover this sensitivity with some insulation so that you can begin to care more about yourself, and less about what other people think of you.

Right now I want you to congratulate yourself for having the capability for such excellent "What if" thinking. It's something you have in common with all of our great artists and scientists. Our forefathers had the courage and imagination to wonder what a new world would be like. Einstein had the curiosity to discover new ways of looking at the universe. Michelangelo could see in a block of marble his statue of David and then proceed to carve it out. Gershwin was able to take the sights and sounds of the streets of Paris and compose *An American in Paris*. The list of opportunities for you to be creative is just as extensive.

The ability to see what might be is a beautiful gift when it's used to create, produce, and expand. It's something you ought to congratulate yourself for. Yet the problem is that you do not use "what if" thinking to create positive new ideas. Too often you're influenced by negative thoughts. You have a tendency to use your creative mind to imagine catastrophes where there aren't any, and see disastrous "maybe" events where only slim possibilities exist. You convince yourself a horrible outcome is inevitable. You say, "I know that I'll make a fool of myself when I try to give that presentation," or, "If the plane hits an air pocket, I'll probably make a spectacle of myself by screaming and running down the aisle."

This is where we have to work toward assisting you to use your creativity and imaginative thinking style to enhance your potential, so you can move successfully toward your goals. You are, like so many fearful people, tricking yourself into believing that people, places, and things really are dangerous and should be avoided at all costs. Or that if you face them, you'll feel overwhelming fear.

Now it's time to begin appreciating your specialness and uniqueness, and to stop evaluating yourself by your anxieties. You are not your fears, anxieties, or phobias! They are merely at this time a part of the total you. Who cares if your knees wobble and feel like gelatin? You'll need to begin to give less power to anxiety and see more strength in yourself. Then you can begin to move ahead with your goals and feel better about yourself.

I want you to keep in mind these four points:

1. Fears and phobias occur to a sensitive person whose imagination works overtime, and who has a way of creating danger where there most likely isn't any.
2. One out of four Americans admits to fears, so the feeling of isolation and alienation that you experience is shared by millions of others.
3. Such fears and phobias are treatable and definitely curable!
4. Instead of kicking yourself for being fearful, start appreciating yourself for your sensitivity and creative "what if" thinking.

Many people are able to mask or avoid their symptoms without others knowing that they actually have a phobia or intense fear. What may appear as the non-fearful person going through life with the greatest of ease, and accomplishing things that seem overwhelming to you, may not be totally true. That person may have perfected the "skill" of avoidance! Or else he or she is so out of touch with feelings nothing and no one matter.

Right now you may be saying to yourself, "Give me one day like that! I'd trade places with that person without blinking an eye!" If you knew the psychological price people like that pay, you may not be so eager to swap. It may be true that now you feel more pain from the anxiety and fear, but it's also true that you feel more happiness, have better relationships, and have more capacity for life all around. So it's actually a packaged deal. Given being a zombie versus being an anxious person (who can conquer his or her anxiety!), most people would choose being the fearful one hands down.

Sally always thought of herself as pretty together and not overly anxious. She was raised in Manhattan with supportive but somewhat overprotective parents, graduated from a prestigious college in the city, and had an excellent position in an advertising firm. Married for four years, she and her husband decided to move to Long Island and buy a home there. Because Sally lived in the city, she never before needed to learn to drive, since a car was inconvenient and unnecessary. Yet most things in the suburbs (trips to the grocery store, access to the train into Manhattan, visiting friends) required driving.

Much to Sally's surprise, learning to drive became an arena for panic. As soon as she got behind the wheel she felt her heart pound and her hands tremble. She would grip the wheel for dear life and pray she would make it home. In the car Sally had one anxiety experience after another.

She began regretting that she moved in the first place and constantly blamed herself for her driving phobia. "How come I have a fear of driving while everyone else seems to approach it with such nonchalance?"

When Sally's driving fear was explored it was discovered that it hardly began when she moved to the suburbs. For about six years she avoided invitations that required her even to be a passenger in a car. She had always rationalized this behavior to herself by saying she had too much work to do over the weekend to go to the Hamptons or upstate. Instead she became an active social hostess to compensate for not accepting those invitations. But after a while her friends became miffed at her reluctance to visit them. Not until Sally took a systematic approach to her fear did she succeed in conquering it. Then her "Why me?" question became "Why did I wait so long?"

Many people who seem just fine indeed may be experts at either avoiding the fear response or haven't had to confront that dreaded situation. I'm saying this to you to help you recognize that fears, anxieties, and phobias affect many people, and as a matter of fact have been around for centuries. It's true that the fears and phobias today may differ from those that people had centuries ago, but they still existed nonetheless. Horse phobias and fears of riding in carriages are really not all that different from present-day fears of traveling in planes, buses, subways, or cars.

Instead of berating yourself with "Why me?" questions it's time to recognize that you're in the company of many talented people who also, at one time or another, felt fear or phobia. Freud had his own fears of travel and heights; William James suffered from acute moments of panic, and so do many brilliant actors and actresses. Although they have enormous self-doubt and performance anxiety, they present themselves as models of poise and excellence.

But such fears do not have to continue to dominate your life! Just as the people I have spoken to you about succeeded and continue to succeed despite their fears, so can you! Each time you start berating yourself with "Why me?" questions, realize that your sensitivity and imagination are strengths. They have led you astray, but only temporarily!

This is what we are going to work on. How to begin a program that stresses what you can do, not what you can't do. Fearful thinking is filled with cautionary words—"Watch out," "You'd better not try," "Be careful!" Such thoughts are designed to strike fear and cause you to do the very thing to perpetuate the feared situation.

The reality is that you can learn to quiet these fears and begin to feel good again. Instead of asking "Why me?" it may be better to ask why you waited so long, and what you can do to tackle the problem. Once you solve it, you won't be asking the question anymore.

CHAPTER TWO

WHAT IS THE FEAR RESPONSE?

THE fear response can hit without warning. You may feel fine one minute; the next moment your mind is racing wildly, your heart is pounding furiously, and all you can think of is ... Escape! Often you keep pushing, but the anxiety you experience leaves you depleted and feeling helpless at times. You feel like running as fast as you can to the nearest exit—out of a restaurant, off an elevator, or out of a lawyer's office where you are about to sign a document. You may be petrified of public speaking, or make your excuses when friends invite you to a singles' get-together. What marks the fear experience is anxiety, sometimes the feeling of paralysis, and then an intense and sudden desire to make a getaway. Or it may cause you to avoid people, places, and things. Whatever the fear, stress accompanies the situation.

These symptoms characterize what I call the *fear response*. As a reaction to certain people, places, objects, or internal physical sensations such as heart palpitations, you feel immense distress ranging from anxiety, to fear, to panic. You feel victimized by your own thoughts and feelings. In the past, you tried to avoid these feelings. But your solution hasn't always worked. That is because the avoidance that you took for something positive and reassuring, has, in fact, done you a lot more harm than you realize. By such avoidance you are making the fear more powerful than you realize, and more intense in the future.

Avoidance is the *bête noire* of fear. Every time you retreat from a source of fear, by leaving a room or refusing to try something, you make it worse the next time. You may kid yourself by believing that what you are doing is safe and reasonable, but it isn't. In fact, just the opposite. Under the influence of the fear, your mind is inviting you to do just what's actually more harmful for you in the long run. It's literally playing tricks on you. It says such things as, "Come on! You know you can't possibly speak out in front of your colleagues. You'll only have a panic attack and make a fool of yourself." "Ride a bus? Who do you think you're kidding?" So you stay away, make excuses, do anything to avoid the fear response.

The anxiety you feel at times of stress can be so painful, it's no wonder you want to avoid it. But I want you to see that in essence your mind is seducing you into believing that you can't do these things. The reality is that from your experiences with anxiety you actually began to believe the catastrophic thoughts. Rather than say, "I'll go to that audition and sing my heart out," you think, "If I go and audition my throat will close up and I'll look like a fool!"

When I say your mind is tricking you, it's because you're seeing things that aren't there. Or if they are, you're seeing them in a very distorted way. Because of your fear, you have trouble distinguishing the reality of the situation. Anxiety colors your life in very negative and restrictive ways.

Part of the challenge we have in front of us is not letting your creative, intelligent mind get the better of you. The dark side of your thinking tells you that every plane trip spells disaster, that each time you try to go above the fourth floor, you'll crumble into a nervous wreck thinking a fire is imminent, or that any time a stranger approaches you for directions you'll be seized by panic.

As a matter of fact, if you suffer from fear, anxiety, or phobias of any kind, think of your mind as a practical joker. It's trying to trick you. It's playing a game with you. It's alarming you, perhaps the way a parent did —"Don't go outside without your umbrella and rubber boots. It might rain." Or, "I don't want you trying out for the team. You may get hurt." Recognize that your own fears are suspect and that they exaggerate the situation; your mind invites the negative thinking associated with fearful thoughts. Unless you realize this, you cheat yourself out of a great deal of freedom and pleasure.

Even before we start, it's important to see exactly what your condition is. I want to give you a brief clinical description of what's happening to you from a psychological point of view. You ought to understand what your body and mind are trying to say to you, especially when you are in the grip of such terrible feelings.

Unfortunately, what's happening now is that your imagination has you seeing tigers where there are merely cuddly kittens. Your imagination, which could be one of your most superb talents, is now your enemy. When it goes wild it can be hurtful. Tigers seem to be closing in. We have to begin to help you to harness that creative energy and have it work for and not against you.

Our ancestors had a wonderful psychological mechanism labeled the "fight or flight" syndrome. Simply stated, this means that when one of our ancient relatives suddenly confronted a tiger at the doorstep of his cave, he had two immediate solutions. Either he could stay and fight it out, or he could run as fast as his legs could carry him. This ability to respond correctly is the exact reason that we're around today to discuss "fight or flight." Obviously they made the right decision! You can thank God your ancestor wasn't one of those nonchalant types who took a look at the tiger and kept munching on a fig leaf. Those characters aren't part of your ancestral heritage and certainly not part of your anxious genes!

When you experience fear or anxiety you feel the same thing that your ancestors felt . . . fight or flee!

When you suffer your own fears, you become subject to the "fight or flight" syndrome. The same sort of bell goes off in your head like the warning that went off millennia ago. Do I stay here and confront the tiger or run away as fast as I can?

Unfortunately, your impulse is usually to flee. But the problem with this kind of response is that each time you run away from the company party, or the checkout line at the supermarket, you're treating that kitten as if it were a tiger! You are in essence seeing these situations as if they were dangerous and to be avoided at all costs. You're seeing danger where there isn't any real threat to your life (the party may be dull or anxiety producing, but a killer it's not!). That's not to say that elevators don't occasionally get stuck, and the clerk in the shopping center isn't sometimes hostile, but they are not life-threatening situations.

In other words, like most anxious people, you have difficulty telling the difference between real and fantasied disaster. This is the key to why your fears, in whatever form they take, seem so scary. You have the power to do "what if" thinking, and that thinking has a tendency to get out of hand. It could be a fear of vomiting in public or shaking during a performance. It could be a fear of blushing in front of co-workers. Nearly everyone lives with fears in some degree. Others may be less a victim than you are, because they have learned to ignore the unreal possibilities. Often they lack the imagination to fear in the first place. The fear response may hit you like a bolt out of the blue. It may not seem connected to anything or anybody, or it may build up gradually over time. Frequently, it strikes its victims without warning, as in spontaneous panic attacks.

Let's step back and look at three distinctions that will be running through this book. The words *fear, anxiety,* and *phobia* are often used interchangeably, but there are important differences. Everyone has some degree of anxiety—before a plane flight, the first day on a new job, speaking out in public. Such anxiety is healthy. It indicates your concern to do and look well. "Show me a player who isn't anxious before a football game and I'll show you a player who doesn't care," is an old sports axiom. You can think of anxiety as geared to the situation you are about to enter. Anxiety is low-level, nervous tension and is more or less accepted by people who feel it.

Fear comes in at a higher level of intensity. Not only are you likely to have physical symptoms, but anticipation shows up as well. Fear begins early, often days before an event. You may be thinking about going into the crowded city during the week, and the previous weekend might be full of fear of getting stuck in traffic, trapped on the bridge, and so on. Fear begins long before the event is to occur, and often builds in intensity.

Phobias are much more specific than fears or anxieties. The terror behind phobias is irrational. There are hints of irrationality behind anxieties and fears, but the dread behind the phobia is so great that the situation is to be avoided at all costs. There is, however, a crucial difference between those who fear and those who are phobic. The fearful person, despite the worry, sweating hands, nervous stomach, and so on, pushes through the situation, whatever it might be. Despite the days of worry, they find themselves on the stage, delivering the speech to the marketing group, or driving into the city.

Despite the fear they do it anyway, albeit with trepidation! But the bottom line is they do it.

The intensity of the fear response is what separates those who feel the usual butterflies in the stomach before giving a presentation from those who experience panic. For some people the reaction to the fear response is enough to make the most heroic shake in their boots. Instead of feeling butterflies before a presentation, the phobic imagines, for example, the very worst that could happen and sees terrible outcomes to a situation. In the same instance a nonphobic person feels a lot of anxiety and might complain about her armpits being drenched, but she doesn't reach the same point of terror.

If you find yourself always imagining that disaster lurks just around the corner, you can then understand why you would start avoiding places and things that cause such painful anxiety. Who in his right mind would want to expose himself to a situation where he expected to tremble, where his heart would pound and legs would turn rubbery—not to mention humiliation at the hands of someone else?

The phobic avoids! It can be done subtly as when someone says, "I'd rather walk. It's such a nice day." Would you ever suspect that person of having a taxi or bus phobia? "The train is so much easier. You can read or just relax." Is that a flying phobia in disguise? Other people find excuses for not attending parties, or perhaps always eating lunch in the office, thus neatly avoiding a restaurant phobia. You'd never suspect that your nextdoor neighbor has trouble making small talk. You just never see her!

Some phobias are free floating, a terror attack that

strikes without warning. Such an attack is called ago-raphobia. Those who are agoraphobic seek the safety of their homes and rarely venture out. To leave the house can be a terrorizing ordeal. Agoraphobia is con-sidered the most intense type of fear because it can strike its victims without any warning, and show up anyplace or anytime.

These distinctions are not airtight. They're merely guidelines to help you separate and emphasize the basic differences. Anxieties are situation-oriented, fears are broader and start earlier, and phobias emphasize flight and avoidance.

You may feel that your symptoms are synonymous with who you are as a person. Yet they actually say so little about you. They're really only a small part of you that has gone astray and causes you to feel conflicted. You could be quite happily married or content to be single. The career you're involved in could be very re-warding and you are probably very successful at it. Although you are constantly aware of your fears, the anxiety problem is not you but rather your creative imagination playing nasty tricks with an otherwise in-telligent brain.

Those feelings are the result of fearing that you could be embarrassed, or feel humiliated, or worse yet, de-stroyed. You've convinced yourself that the anxiety you experience is self-protective, and acts as a shield to a greater disaster. Let's consider how your imagination is working against you, producing such horrendous di-sasters as:

1. "I know if I fly from New York to Washington the plane will never make it" (even though a

large number of planes fly there daily without any problem).

2. "If I enter a supermarket, I'll feel jittery and my heart will pound, my legs will feel weak, and I'll absolutely have to run as fast as I can." The reality is that no one has X-ray vision to see whether your heart is pounding or your legs are rubbery.

3. "If I drive on the freeway I know my car will lose control and smash into a concrete barrier." Yet the fact is that you've driven for years before your fear and never had an accident.

4. "If I leave the house, I'll probably collapse or faint." But having never fainted before, the likelihood is rare.

5. "If I have to go to the fiftieth floor I'll probably be terrified, and look it too!" Yet people in the elevator are more concerned with their upcoming business.

All these thoughts are negative in nature and have awful, catastrophic consequences. They are dominated by negative "what if" thinking. The examples are indicative of your rich imagination—but an imagination that is working overtime and against you. Your fears prevent you from being able to think rationally in a phobic situation. Instead of saying to yourself, "It's possible that the elevator may get stuck," start using your imagination to consider the number of elevators that carry millions of people every day without getting stuck. The likelihood of it happening is rather slim.

This is where I want to help you to slowly take the steps necessary to overcome the fear response. Think about the thousands of people who have sucessfully dealt with their fears, anxieties, and phobias. People throughout the world are now living a life free from such feelings that plagued them previously.

I almost hear you saying to yourself, "Yes, but my fears and anxieties seem too big to conquer. I can't possibly do this," or, "But I've had them for so long. They're a part of me that I can't change." That's your negative imagination talking again. Such resistance to imagining a life free from fear is very natural at this point. How can you expect to feel otherwise when the anxiety has a way of making you feel so helpless and hopeless?

Let's begin by introducing some new questions to ask yourself. Try, "Why shouldn't I be able to join all those other people who have successfully overcome their fears and anxieties?" There's no reason why you can't work through and overcome your fears exactly the same way so many other people have. You could have picked up another book, but instead you are saying, "I want to get past these fears and stop them from ruling my life." Just reading this book shows motivation, determination, and discipline. This says a lot about you, and such qualities are important to defeat the fantasied fears.

We have to start demystifying your fears, anxieties, and phobias so that their power over you diminishes. I'm going to give you a brief history of those feelings and then explain to you the various types, so that you can start by understanding more about the clinical nature of the fear response.

Together we are going to explore alternative ways of thinking about your fears, so that you can break out of the negative pattern you're now in. You can begin to move forward and overcome your fears, anxieties, and phobias in whatever form they take or whatever arena they're played out. The time has come to stop allowing these ideas to rule your life. You are a victim of your own imagination. Instead of looking for catastrophic endings to a scenario, you are going to use your talents to imagine more realistic successes.

Overcoming the fear response will take discipline, commitment, and a lot of initial risks. But you can take these steps at your own pace. It's important not to burden yourself with unnecessary baggage by saying, "It's time to stop acting stupid. Just get on that plane and fly!" or, "What's wrong with me that I climb fifteen stories instead of using the elevator?" Self-blame isn't going to be helpful to you. In fact, it's part and parcel of the problem. And when you can stop that, you've taken a big step toward overcoming your fear.

CHAPTER THREE

YOUR
CREATIVE
IMAGINATION

Anxiety is the essential condition of intellectual and artistic creation, and everything that is finest in human history.

—Charles Frankel

BELIEVE it or not, it's your highly attuned creativity that has a way of working against you. In other words, your very best friend, your originality and ability to create new ideas, has a way of leading you astray. But creativity isn't such a great friend when your fearful imagination runs wild, and "what if" thinking takes charge!

Your imagination allows you to realize your hopes, dreams, and aspirations. Without seeing possibilities of what could be, you wouldn't be where you are in work and personal relationships. Yet that same gift also presents obstacles to you. That same thinking process has a way of putting up barriers toward achieving those dreams.

To be able to be futuristically oriented in your thinking gives you the opportunity to see potentials where other people see nothing, or are oblivious to the outcome. Sounds great . . . unless you are a fearful person whose imagination has a way of spelling disaster. Instead of thinking of all the best possibilities that lie ahead, you tend to see the worst possible thing that could happen. Then you act *as if* it were true.

This sort of thinking besets all those with fears and anxieties, and in many ways intimidates them. With people who have simple fears and phobias, the elevator going from the first to the fifth floor spells disaster. "It'll get stuck" you may think, "I'll never be able to climb through the rescue hatch in the ceiling." Your every vision is of being powerless and helpless. Your heart races and your mind rushes from one bad ending to another. You imagine being trapped for hours, or the cable snapping and the elevator plunging downward.

With airline fears, simply boarding a plane can be a nightmare. Peter, a successful engineer, worked for a large insurance company as an inspector. The headquarters were located in Chicago, which was only a half-hour drive for Peter, who lived in an outlying suburb. One day, his boss congratulated him on being chosen to represent the firm at the annual meeting in San Francisco. It meant a promotion and a substantial raise. But the promotion also brought with it travel requirements and Peter suffered from a severe flying fear.

Peter was terrified. The realization that he would have

to fly regularly was utterly dismaying. The first scheduled trip to San Francisco felt like torture. He found out about it on a Friday and was to set out the following Monday. He told his secretary to make all the arrangements and tried to forget about it. He would be traveling first class with all of the amenities possible. In addition he booked himself into a marvelous hotel suite, so that he would have something to look forward to. Still he was miserable! In his search to find a rational basis for his fears, he scoured the newspapers all weekend for any news of airline crashes. He began to listen to news broadcasts expecting to hear of an airline disaster. At this point his creative imagination went into overdrive. Without any evidence he argued with his wife on the unreliability of flying, rejecting whatever logic she used in an attempt to assuage his fears. The more she said, the angrier he got. So what if planes took off and landed safely hundreds of times a day. Accidents did happen, and he still had the flight ahead of him. Logic and reality don't mean a hill of beans when personal safety is involved. Arguments that present the facts—for instance, that flying is safer than driving—fall on deaf ears.

Peter's ability to visualize and think creatively was a real talent on the job. His expertise was recognized and rewarded by his promotion. Yet that same gift was disastrous for his fears. It was one thing to consider potential accidents; it was something else to visualize every plane trip as the end. Peter imagined only the very worst and convinced himself that he'd never make it. He toyed with the notion of confessing his fears to his boss, but was afraid it would jeopardize his new position. He felt totally helpless.

The following is a typical example of simple fearful

thinking: believing that disasters and catastrophes are imminent and will most certainly happen to you. The only way you can escape the fear is to avoid putting yourself in the situation in the first place.

The problem with this false thinking is that it restricts rather than expands your life. It severly limits your ability to move ahead. You say to yourself, "I know that the subway will get stuck between stops," or, "I'm sure the elevator won't make it, the cables will break and I'll be trapped inside." You imagine that bridges will surely collapse if you cross them; tunnels will flood when you are halfway through them, and then you'll drown in your car; or that you'll get swallowed up by an escalator as it slowly approaches its floor.

Fearful people expend energy on imagining that if something's possible then it will certainly happen—no questions asked! I suppose that with the exception of the escalator swallowing you up all the other scenarios are remotely possible. Yet in reality all of these horrors are highly improbable. The fault of such thinking is that it doesn't respond to logical reasoning. As the brilliant English philosopher David Hume once said, "Reason is always the slave of the Passions!" Thus your creative imagination sees all sorts of probabilities where only vague, infrequent possibilities exist. Your feelings, not your reason, dictate to you.

All fearful people have this in common. They focus their energy on believing that they will never recover from a faux pas in public. God forbid someone saw them blush or tremble when they signed the check. If anyone did, they may as well pack it in! Life is one series of fantasied social screw-ups after another.

When this happens, you will naturally find a problem

in distinguishing reality from fantasy. You are creative, but in a curious sense, too creative. I am going to show you how you can use your creativity to rescue you from the fears and phobias rather than to deepen the problem and make it worse.

You may imagine yourself vomiting in a restaurant, frantically clawing at a revolving door that gets jammed, or jumping out of your car if you are mired in traffic. In all cases you will feel terribly humiliated afterward. This is the imaginative skill of the fearful person. But this "skill" prevents the person from recognizing his or her strengths and talents.

Kim worked as an administrative assistant for a large bank. She hated being asked to lunch for fear that her hands wouldn't be able to pick up her food without trembling, and that everyone would notice and think there was something wrong. She constantly made excuses about why she had to work through lunch, and would buy a sandwich to have at her desk with nothing whatsoever to drink. She imagined that the sandwich was "heavier" than a salad (which she preferred), and judged her eating habits on how heavy something was. The more leverage she imagined, the less shaking would occur. After lunch, Kim would bolt for the water fountain to avoid the hiccups that always seemed to result from eating a sandwich quickly, without anything to drink.

Life for Kim became a constant avoidance of eating in social situations. After a while she dreaded being asked to lunch even with friends. She felt too embarrassed to tell them her problem. Around holiday time, when the people from her office would meet for a drink after work, Kim's anxiety skyrocketed. She made excuses, and if pressured to go, went and ordered exotic drinks with long straws, thus avoiding picking up the glass and bringing it to her mouth. You can see how Kim let her imagination control her behavior.

This is one way that your creativity heightens your fears: the intense belief that what you imagine will in fact happen and humiliate you in front of others. You are afraid that you'll look like a fool at an audition, miss your lines, and be taken off the stage a shaking mess. Or if you try to give a presentation in front of other salespeople you will humiliate yourself in public. The audience will begin to whisper to each other and shuffle in their seats.

With such fears and phobias your creative energy works overtime. Danger lurks everywhere and anywhere! Worse yet, such fears can reach the panic stage. For some, when they least expect or anticipate it, panic appears. The excruciating torture of panic spasms that accompany the fear response is enough to frighten a four-star general. The pounding heart, jelly legs that seem to give them the feeling that they can't carry themselves another step, shaking hands, and dizziness are all powerful scary symptoms that can strike them anywhere and at any time—in a shopping mall or driving, or even leaving the house. This is now the realm of the phobic. Is it any wonder that phobics feel that the world is a scary place to venture out into? And all of this is due to an overactive imagination.

You're walking down the street and without warning a neighbor appears and wants to tell you about her son's nursery school experience. As soon as you spot her, your mind starts conjuring up excuses for getting away as soon as politely possible. The last thing you need at this point is to have to talk to someone when you woke up with that queasy, anxious feeling. You know all too well what the anxious feeling is signaling you about. Whenever you wake up with it in the pit of your stomach you know the day will be one fearful moment after another. Your imagination starts dreading the day ahead and creates the worst possible scenarios.

Audrey, a professor of English, had her first panic attack when she approached her chairperson to change her schedule. She was constantly given the worst schedule in the department. She'd spent two years of teaching eight o'clock classes on Monday mornings and four o'clock classes on Friday afternoons, while everyone else in the department had a more convenient schedules. She decided to request different class times. Her chairman was an incredibly hostile and envious man in his mid-fifties who hadn't published an article in five years, whereas Audrey had published articles over the last ten years in prestigious journals. Because he resented her abilities, he decided to use his power against her when drawing up her schedule.

Audrey asked for an appointment to see him. She gently but assertively asked whether her schedule could be changed for the next semester, since lecturing at the times assigned left her little time for writing.

Her chairman became furious and informed her that she had no right even to ask that, since she was hired as an assistant professor and others had more seniority. In fact, Audrey has seniority over three of the people in her department. Nonetheless, they got the better schedules.

Here we have an attractive, intelligent woman, well respected by her colleagues and students. Yet like so many creative people, panic suddenly seized her. Her attacks began suddenly and without warning approximately a year and a half ago. Audrey can vividly describe the incident with painstaking detail. While Audrey's chairman was "explaining" to her why it was impossible to give her better time slots, her mind suddenly went blank, her throat closed up, and she thought she couldn't speak. Her hands trembled furiously and she wanted to run as far from him as possible.

Actually what Audrey was experiencing was a "rage" attack. But she experienced these feelings as panic! She was so furious at this hostile, withholding, competitive man that her only recourse at that moment was to defend herself from her rage by anxiety.

Audrey could visualize what she looked like during the anxiety attack and felt that it was also visible to him. *The problem with a creative imagination is that you can visually picture how you look and what people think about your anxiety!*

To direct your imagination to work for you will require effort, particularly if you are accustomed to seeing crouching lions instead of friendly kittens. But what do we know about you?

Fact #1: Anxious people are among the most creative people around. Fearful and phobic thinking can be exhausting and require a great deal of energy, so much that it sometimes seems too painful to bear. Yet you do bear it, which is a sign of your strength!

Fact #2. Fearful thinking actually requires a great deal of rich imagination, which is terribly helpful when pursuing artistic inventions. Yet it's not such a great friend when your fearful imagination runs wild and "what if" thinking takes charge!

Yet think of how exhilarating it would feel to harness that power and have it on your side. To help you avoid being stuck in "what if" negative thinking, I'm going to show you how to break out of this fear mode, use your creative energy effectively, and make it serve you to move ahead and be less fearful!

CHAPTER FOUR

THE INNER VOICES OF FEAR

> Superstition is a premature explanation that overstays its time.
>
> —George Iles

PEOPLE with strong anxieties often think alike. Many have an inner voice spelling disaster at every turn. This voice is relentless, and clouds their judgment whenever they contemplate moving ahead. If the intensity of the inner voice becomes too strong, people either practice avoidance or use "magical" rituals to ward off the fear. Superstitions run rampant and exert enormous control over their lives. Such people erroneously believe if they utilize rituals or obsessive thinking patterns, their fears and phobias will be kept at bay. Let's examine both of these ways of dealing with fears.

"There's absolutely no way I can push through my stage nerves this time and go to that audition."

"Even the thought of getting stuck in traffic makes me break out in a cold sweat!"

"You've got to be kidding! Me walk into that crowded department store and buy a blouse. With all those people waiting in line before me? Hah! That'll be the day!"

These typical fears are known as catastrophic thinking patterns. The problem is that when you get caught in the throes of these thoughts, you can't even imagine doing the thing you want most to do. The very thought itself makes you shake inside. The inner monologue of the fearful and phobic person is punctuated with references like "I can't," "I'll look like a fool," and "Everyone will see how anxious I am." Constant negative forebodings mar your day and interfere with your ability to enjoy life fully.

Your inner voice is negative and strives to have you defeat yourself by not trying. It yells "AVOID! RUN! HIDE! GIVE UP!" It tells you that "You can't possibly go to that shopping mall. You'll get dizzy and faint and look like a real jerk in front of hundreds of people." Or "Who, *you*? Drive a car across that bridge? *Never!*"

For example, Jane, a bright, attractive women in her mid-thirties, sold computers for a prestigious multinational firm. She had a fine mathematical mind and constantly read the research in her field. As a sales representative she was required to give speeches four times a year to roomfuls of people, in different cities across the world. Yet she dreaded public speaking like the plague. This was her personal nightmare that constantly haunted her. Weeks before a scheduled speech, pessimistic thoughts flooded her mind. She imagined colleagues seeing her anxiety and then judging her as inept and making snide comments behind her back. She feared humiliation at the hands of an aggressive sales manager, who would leap at the chance to embarrass her for her imagined quivering voice and trembling hands. In her mind she would picture herself at the podium blushing and stuttering as she managed to squeak out a few words. "What happens if this time I collapse, or the anxiety gets so intolerable that I have to run out of the room shaking in my boots? I'd be so disgraced I'd have to quit my job."

Such visions and thoughts would beset her in the shower or driving to work—in fact in any solitary moment. The very anticipation would make her feel dizzy. The gist of her conclusions were always the same: "I can't do it. I'll have to quit before I make a complete ass of myself."

Every attempt by her husband to reassure her failed. "Forget it! It's all in your imagination. You can do it. You've done it before. What's the big deal?" But his words fell on deaf ears—ears too long accustomed to hearing words of disaster.

You, like Jane, may constantly imagine that whenever you confront the feared situation, disaster lurks, ready to pounce. When you become aware of your inner dialogue you start to become sensitive to the messages your mind sends to you. You may even find that its tone is all too familiar, reminding you of someone else's voice. You start hearing the words as those of someone in your past or present—a parent for example. Perhaps your mother was always cautioning you every time you set foot out of the house. Some parents may inadvertently create a vision of a world that's replete with danger. Instead of encouraging the child to take healthy risks, they throw scary notions at them: "Watch out for this" and "Be careful of that" are peppered throughout their speech. Or perhaps, even today, friends say, "The competition is awfully stiff. I wouldn't even bother trying out for that job if I were you."

The list of disastrous adjectives a fearful person has at his or her disposal is endless. All these words are designed to describe the situation in the worst possible way. Neutral terms don't seem to exist when you confront your fears. Nor do any hopeful, nurturing, or encouraging words. Fear awaits you, ready to spring like a ferocious animal when you think about giving a speech, taking a bus, going to an interview, boarding a plane, or even entering a relationship. You feel victimized and helpless, not knowing what to do. To confront your fears seems to invite danger. The warning voice screams out at you: "What if the elevator gets stuck? Will there be enough air?" To enter an office party by yourself is sheer torture. To be fearful means imagining impending doom in certain situations and the worst possible scenario.

I want you to become aware of how these messages are instructing you to feel and react. Note that thinking, "Oh my God, I'll be trapped in a crowd and won't be able to breathe. I'm better off staying at home" is setting yourself up for the fear response. Such thinking leaves you with nothing but anxiety and hopelessness.

As you become more sensitive to the inner voice and just how you work yourself up, you will become aware of what you are saying to yourself. By tuning into the internal sentences you can start to change how you look at your fears. You can begin to alter the negative force of your brain, and function on a less anxious level. The chemicals in the brain are controlled by your view of the world. You want to release the tranquil chemicals, such as serotonin, through positive internal sentences. This way you can find peace and serenity instead of fear and trepidation. And you can begin to separate your fears from those of someone else that you now call your own. Just because a parent or sibling or some other significant person feared interviews doesn't mean you also have to.

Under the spell of such thinking, you probably feel it's impossible to go on and survive the anxiety or the panic spasms without imminent disaster lurking at the end. Whether it's giving a presentation as in Jane's case or going to a singles get-together all alone, the thoughts are always those of a doomsayer.

Your aim must be to change the inner voice, to instruct yourself to think positively and start to silence that negative voice. Of course, this is going to take time, as anything worthwhile does. But remember, it took years of conditioning to make you believe such disasters are imminent. So it will take you a while to see that not only are your goals within reach but also that your fears are imaginary. Just remember that millions of people have suffered fears and have overcome them in the past, and that millions more will work toward overcoming them in the future.

I'm going to show you how to restructure that inner voice so that it ceases to be pessimistic. You'll learn how to start programming yourself differently. I want you to move toward a newly found vocabularly free from catastrophe!

Other fearful people are driven by magical rituals and superstitions to stave off disaster. Spurred on by an overactive imagination, fearful thinking takes on a life all its own. Such thinking is apt to seem illogical to anyone not predisposed to anxiety or phobias. Nonetheless, you may say, "So what if thousands of planes successfully take off daily, or millions of people take the subway or cross a bridge. I'll be the exception. My time will be up, I just know it."

The fearful mind often seeks to stave off such disasters with magical thoughts or with rituals, designed to keep danger away. These rituals can become what psychologists call obsessional thinking, and alas, it plagues many fearful people and causes them undue stress.

Your impulse may tell you to try anything, even if it seems silly, in order to stay in a state of safety. You may avoid driving or scheduling meetings on certain days of the month, or perhaps you won't stay in hotel rooms with particular numbers. To your way of thinking, the price of inconvenience is small considering that it may be a life or death situation.

For many people, even the act of thinking itself can seem hazardous. If they think of someone or something abhorrent, then they need to erase that thought immediately. Not to do so means that danger will surely follow.

This thinking is inhibiting, since their minds desperately seek to find a positive association, in the belief that they can ward off a looming terror. Yet such rituals do not deal with the underlying feelings behind the obsession. They accomplish nothing in the long run except to keep those who practice them busy pretending.

Andy feared passing a funeral procession. His mind raced, imagining the worst fate that would befall him if he even glanced at the row of cars across the street. What if he caught "dead germs," he would think. He desperately tried to evoke memories of people who could protect him and ward off his doom. He held his breath, afraid to breathe the air near someone who was dead. He mistakenly believed that if he saw a funeral, he would certainly die. He would pretend to himself that he didn't see the funeral procession, and looked at everything but the cars lined up.

Since this imaginary causal pattern is always of a horrible nature, it must be offset by avoidance, both physical and mental. A second line of defense is calling upon protective spirits.

Fearful people shun everything that even hints at catastrophe. A hospital, a doctor's office, and all other feared environments are to be avoided because of what might happen. Reality means nothing. The probability of a dangerous event occuring is irrelevant.

Why do people engage in such thinking? For many it is a holdover from childhood, where it was frequently practiced. When we were children the world was a scary place indeed. Between spiders, the dark, thunderstorms, and the like, we felt helpless and frightened out of our wits. We had no control whatsoever, and could be the victim of dangerous forces. "Any disturbance in the process of the child's adaptation to reality at any stage of his intellectual development can lead to the formation of neurotic responses, and these responses are carried into adulthood."[1]

The child "is neither able to define objects correctly, nor explain the causes of actions or events. He has not yet developed the mental capacity to see the relationship between cause and effect."[2] The child is unable to distinguish between his subjective emotional experiences and the objective laws governing reality. Magical thinking becomes the means of dealing with this conflict.

Whenever Bob crossed the bridge between Oakland and San Francisco, he felt he had to protect himself by thinking of certain forces that could assist him. He evoked their names, just as he did as a child. "Please God, be with me today." What he was trying to avoid was his unfounded fear of the bridge collapsing.

Cathy feared that any negative thought she had at the time her husband was hammering a nail into a wall would be permanently added to the house. She had to flee the room, desperately filling her mind with positive thoughts that would protect herself and her husband from disaster.

In other words, some adults retain, in certain areas of their thinking, childish levels of belief that affect the interpretation of reality. A vicious circle is created. The fear of the event or object or thought produces anxiety, which in turn leads to the avoidance of the feared object. But the true threat is never tested, and its avoidance is supported by a judgmental confusion between imagined disaster and the true situation.[3]

This confusion between reality and imagination continues into adulthood, and is constantly reinforced by the responses of the autonomic nervous system.[4] When the autonomic nervous system goes into high gear, your body reacts automatically to stress and causes you to respond immediately. You may feel somewhat faint as the blood rushes from your head, or your hands suddenly perspire. Your heart can act like a trip hammer. This is your involuntary "autonomic" nervous system responding to anxiety. The fear increases in intensity. Soon the person perceives that he or she cannot control the specific anxiety situation because they cannot control their physical feelings.

There is also an opposite reaction for some children whose fears increase the sensitivity of the autonomic system, thus developing an intensity of feelings beyond what other people feel in the same situation. Thus sensitive children become more sensitive, and in some cases, become prone to the fear response.

The anxiety produced by a specific situation is "unexplainable fear."[5] Thus the panic that is set off when such a person sees a dog or cat is not only irrational, but involves physiological reactions. The body produces the fight or flight symptoms. Some people realize that the fear is silly, but they cannot stop their reaction when the situation arises. Magical thinking is the attempt to control forces that they believe will destroy them. It's really an attempt to deal with helplessness and pretend that they are in control after all.

It's rather understandable to see how these magical rituals would be evoked. The world, to many fearful people, is a scary place. Just turn on a news broadcast or pick up a newspaper or magazine and you're involved in terrorism, earthquakes, murders, and other assorted violence. Or talk to a neighbor and hear about who's got what disease and is dying. Isn't it understandable that we would want to resort to some magical thoughts to make the world safer?

Magical rituals have been around since the world began. Wearing crosses, carrying lucky charms, or attempting to know the future by reading a daily horoscope are attempts to ward off disaster. Going to expensive spas that claim healing powers and drinking from the fountain of youth are efforts to gain some control over our lives.

Helplessness is one of the worst feelings imaginable to both humans and animals. The cries of a cat trapped in a tree, or of a dog stuck in a closet, show us that this is a universal fear. Helplessness brings out primitive fears that fearful people desperately attempt to deal with, by either avoidance or magic. They make irrational connections where there aren't any, see magical solutions where logic and reality should abound, and feel dominated by superstition.

If you find yourself involved in any magical thinking rituals, it will be important to move toward more constructive thought and action patterns. I want to help

you deal with your surroundings through real probabilities, instead of imagined possibilities. In later chapters I will assist you in seeing the world through your
strengths and help you avoid catering to your fantasied
fears.

CHAPTER FIVE

HOW FEARS, ANXIETIES, AND PHOBIAS DOMINATE YOUR LIFE

IT'S horrible when you think of all the verbal commands you give to yourself when it comes to fears and anxieties. The words you use even when fantasizing driving on the freeway are, as we have seen, filled with disasters. Now it's time to look more closely at how these words affect your behavior.

The reality is that the more you speak to yourself,

the more constricted your life will be. Dave is a good example of what can happen when anxieties dominate one's thinking. Here it was a warm, sunny day in June. Ordinarily Dave would have felt great, but that day he had a big meeting scheduled with his boss, who picks up flaws as if examining with a jeweler's loupe. Dave had been rehearsing the meeting in his mind as he went to work in the morning. He headed for his favorite coffee shop and thought it would be nice to see some of the regulars. As he stepped inside he felt a wave of uneasiness creep over him. At the counter, the waitress put his usual cup of coffee and Danish in front of him, and was talking about the weather, but he couldn't really hear her. His mind started to go blank.

Suddenly he felt disoriented and his heart was pounding. He desperately tried to control himself, but as he picked up the cup, he spilled coffee on the counter. He put his shaking hands on his lap. All he could think of was, "What the hell is happening? Am I losing it? I've got to get out of here!"

He fumbled some change onto the counter and bolted for the door. On the street, things seemed a little better. But what in God's name happened? One thing is certain: he didn't want a repeat performance! Now he was feeling very stressed and he had to go to work.

As he entered the building he suddenly thought of the upcoming meeting. What if those horrible feelings seized him during the meeting? It's one thing to look foolish in front of your morning cronies. It's quite another to look that way with your boss and co-workers present. He knew his job could be on the line.

Fortunately, those feeling didn't arise and his presentation went smoothly. But that didn't calm his fears.

The next day, when he passed the coffee shop again, he decided *not* to go in. He hurried past so that his friends wouldn't see him, telling himself there wasn't time for breakfast. He had to finish that report on his desk. Again and again, he avoided going in. After a while he never went back.

There was a real loss involved. He enjoyed the interlude with those friends. But the thought of having another attack was terrifying and potentially humiliating. Not only was he deprived of a pleasure, he felt foolish. He ruminated about what they must be thinking about him. He felt enormous anxiety in the pit of his stomach everytime he thought that someone might have noticed his attack. The question ran through his mind, "What's wrong with me? I can't even go into a stupid luncheonette." By now he was avoiding the coffee shop as if it were a mine field. And in a sense it was.

Actually his own avoidance had been crucial in building his fear to the height it was now at. *Avoidance is the fuel for the fear response!* Every time you avoid a fearful situation, object, or person, you reinforce your fear.

Such fearful thoughts have a way of dominating your life and interfering with your creative potential. They also interfere with successful relationships and careers. Brenda, a gifted actress in her late twenties, dreads auditions. As soon as she knows that one is scheduled she starts the fear cycle. She begins to worry that she's not good enough and that she'll never get a call-back. As a result of this she turns down lots of chances for furthering her career by avoiding auditions that would enhance her opportunities.

Ken, an attractive single man in his early thirties, is phobic about social situations. He hates the singles scene because he feels extremely anxious whenever he has to talk to a woman. He starts to perspire and he feels his heart beating faster than usual. He feels that he's going to become tongue-tied and that the woman will think he's unattractive because she'll spot his anxiety. So instead of Ken becoming involved in a relationship, he's more involved with his own thoughts of fear, which dominate his actions.

In order to stop giving power to your fears you have to be prepared to take risks and move beyond the scope of those feelings.

1. *Avoidance is the best friend of the fear response!* This means that when you continue to avoid those people, places, or things that you dread you reinforce your fear or phobia and strenghten its hold on you.

2. *You can take the steps as slowly as needed.* To break the fear-avoidance pattern takes time, so you don't have to expect an overnight cure. Just as it took time to develop a phobia by practicing the avoidance technique, so it will take some doing to unlearn a fear or phobia. Taking risks involves some practice, and you need to be kind to yourself during this period.

3. *As you begin to challenge the fear response, give yourself credit for your courage.* I can assure you

that *anyone* who experienced such anxiety would naturally start to avoid the things that caused it. Isn't it natural to want to stay away from something that produces such painful feelings? That's why when you start to confront situations that cause high levels of anxiety you really are showing strength of character and the real essence of who you are.

4. *Acknowledge that it may be impossible not to have setbacks at times. Setbacks are part of the human condition.* You've heard of that saying, "Two steps forward, one step backward." There's always trial and error; sometimes you'll win against your fears and sometimes they'll have the upper hand. The important thing is that you continue to try and win over your fears, despite temporary setbacks. Depression and hopelessness sometimes accompany setbacks, but you'll triumph in the end.

5. *The fear response is something that you can temper in time. Ultimately, those shouts of "watch out!" will become a faint echo.* I'm going to show you how to focus more on the opportunities that await you when you take elevators, drive, speak in public, dine in restaurants, and stop avoiding leaving the house for fear of panic. Imagine walking into a department store without the usual jitters. It will happen!

When Eileen first came to me she was afraid of crossing bridges and going through tunnels. She was an extremely talented executive for an advertising agency in New Jersey. Eileen admitted her fears and realized that she was restricting her life, since she didn't attend the plays and movies she wanted to see, or visit with friends in the city. She knew that if she worked across the Hudson River, in New York City, her salary would take a jump by $20,000. She recognized that it was time for her to do something about her fears and was determined to work at overcoming them.

Eileen can still vividly recall the trepidation and sweating palms as she attempted driving on the George Washington Bridge for the first time. She was so scared her heart felt like it was going two hundred beats a minute. She was convinced she couldn't make it. I had told her to call me as soon as she got to the entrance to the bridge. We spoke briefly and it was clear that she was scared but was going to make it. Trembling hands and all, she paid her toll and proceeded across the Hudson. On the other side she called me again and was ecstatic! "I did it! I'm in New York!"

Each trip became easier until finally the fear response was no longer. The internal words "You can't" became remote memories belonging to a distant past. Eileen now works for a prestigious advertising agency in Manhattan, and never gives the bridge or tunnel a second thought.

This is the kind of experience you too can have when your fears and phobias become minimal in your life. Instead of having these feelings restrict and limit your opportunities, you will start to see possibilities all over the place. A new world will open doors for you that you felt were previously closed.

Dining in restaurants, traveling, signing your name in public, public speaking—all these can be done! Instead of dreading these events you start looking forward to them. It doesn't have to be a dream beyond your reach. Instead, you can make it a part of your everyday reality.

CHAPTER SIX

THE ANNOYANCE
OF SIMPLE FEARS
AND PHOBIAS

SIMPLE fears and phobias are those related to specific objects. These fearful situations can range from seeing a cat to sailing on a ship to hearing a thunderstorm. You may become anxious at the sight of an escalator or revolving door. God forbid you're asked to a roof-top dinner if you hate heights. The symptoms are those that occur with all fearful people: sweating palms, trembling knees, dryness in the throat, racing heart, dizziness.

Specific fears may be of flying or driving, they may

be animal or insect phobias, or they may be about certain everyday occurrences. This fear disorder can be simply a nuisance or it can affect you in ways that you find acutely distressful.

You are walking down a familiar street looking in some store windows. Suddenly, you see a neighbor out mowing his lawn and the sight of the lawnmower seizes you with terror. Your heart starts racing, palms sweat, knees tremble. You've got to get out of here! Is it the particular person who causes this reaction, or some bad memory? Actually, it is the sight of that lawnmower and your dread of it. You remember having heard as a child that someone's foot was severed by a lawnmower, and you never forgot it. Specific situations are automatic triggers. They push your fight or flight buttons and you immediately react. Even though the memory was from your childhood, the anxiety is present today. That's why you need to deal with its importance to you now.

As I've said, simple fears may be either a minor inconvenience or affect you in a way that's highly restrictive. If you have children or friends who want you to visit them in California, and you live in Pennsylvania and have a flying fear, it could be a real problem.

Mark is a vice-president for a bank in Houston. His daughter lives with her husband in London and recently had her first baby. She very much wanted to have her parents visit her, but Mark had a severe flying phobia. His daughter knew of his fear, but didn't want to fly to visit her parents while the baby was so young. Mark's wife, Nancy, was also phobic about flying, so that they never visited their daughter, who had lived in England for five years.

This is an example of how a "simple" phobia becomes

a lot more complex. In this case, there were hurt and angry feelings on the part of the daughter, who didn't understand what the big deal was to make one trip. And Mark and Nancy felt humiliation and guilt.

It is natural to feel some anxiety when one is looking over the edge of a tall building. But when the area is totally enclosed, and there's a plate glass window for protection, the nonfearful person feels safe. He or she may even casually look over the edge! Not so for the person with specific fears. Even though there's no actual danger, his or her knees tremble as if the building will collapse, or the plate glass window will somehow mysteriously give way.

Michael had a real fear of heights. The mere thought of taking an elevator to observation decks of tall buildings was enough to cause him severe panic. Yet one day he was forced to go to a restaurant at the top of a skyscraper and entertain clients from out of town, who were eager to see the San Francisco skyline.

He tried not to think about it as the elevator sped to the top. The muscles of his calves began contracting. His face wore a fixed smile and his responses were minimal. At the top he forced his trembling legs to carry him to the table and chose a seat facing away from the windows. The panic symptoms subsided somewhat as he got involved in the conversation, but immediately returned as lunch was finished and the group headed for the elevator. Once on the ground a wave of relief swept over him and he felt immensely better. The ordeal was over, but he realized he needed to seek treatment for the fear, since such lunches were likely to occur again.

Animals and insects are common stimuli for simple

fears and phobias. The sight of a spider can make you run as fast as you can. Heights, closed spaces, water, lightning and thunder—not to mention flying or driving—all can trigger the fear response. But simple fears and phobias have an advantage over other fears. Since affected people are aware of their fear, they can take steps to avoid it, and with great subtlety. These people usually lead relatively normal lives. They can disguise their fears with claims of preference and choice so that even their friends often fail to observe that they're practicing avoidance. "I'd rather not take the touring bus today. I'm tired of sightseeing," one might say—and a trip to the top of a tall building is neatly avoided. "The subways seem so inefficient. Why don't we take a cab?" another might suggest. And who could recognize a subway phobia? Yet for some, avoidance and excuses are not possible, so they take measures to minimize their fears. It's not coincidental that some people will refuse hotel rooms above the third floor, thus having an easy escape in case of fire.

Just imagine for a moment being trapped in an elevator on your way to work, while your heart races and your perspiration comes down in bucketfuls and the other people around you are using up all your air! Some people can imagine this all too well. And that thought is enough to make that person avoid such an experience and take the stairs.

If you suffer from a simple fear or phobia, then you know all too well that your fear hits whenever you confront the feared situation. If you're afraid of heights and can avoid them, that's one thing. But when you can't, as in Michael's case, you'll feel the old bugaboo of anxiety and be frightened for your life.

Roger ran a camera shop in a popular shopping mall. He was personable and up on all the latest cameras, films, and lenses. But if a customer walked into the store with a dog, Roger froze. His throat immediately went dry and he broke out into a sweat. If his assistant was there, Roger could flee into the back room. But if he was alone, he had to deal with the customer. He always felt humiliated after the customer left, never knowing if he sounded coherent or not. He wondered whether the customer knew about his fears, which also made him upset.

As you can see, or may know already, simple fears and phobias are focused on objects or situations. When confronted with a dreaded situation the fearful person will react with all the fear symptoms. Afterward, in his or her more rational moments, that person can never understand why such events were so terrifying. But such people have an advantage over other phobics in that they know how to avoid the feared situation. Other people, as we shall see in the next two chapters, are not so fortunate.

CHAPTER SEVEN

HOW SOCIAL FEARS AND PHOBIAS INTERFERE WITH RELATIONSHIPS

SOCIAL fears and phobias can be downright embarrassing. Take blushing for example. Laura, a twenty-year-old secretary for a large toy manufacturer, was sitting at her desk when Jim, a handsome salesman for the company, approached her to discuss some work. Laura instantly felt the blood rush to her face and neck. She knew she was probably crimson and felt vulnerable and humiliated. To make matters worse, although Jim didn't mention a thing, some of the other secretaries teased her about the incident. This can be devastating to someone who blushes. Now Laura felt even worse, since her blushing was "public."

Laura had a history of blushing when she was younger but it hadn't affected her for a few years now. After the incident with Jim, she began to worry obsessively that it might recur. This is the essence of social fears and phobias. It's the feeling that you'll look like a fool in front of everyone else. It's an interactional phobia based on your image of yourself, as well as how you imagine other people think and feel about you.

For some people, eating and drinking in public is the source of tremendous anxiety. They imagine that they won't be able to pick up a glass without their hands trembling noticeably. Or worse, they'll vomit from anxiety. For others just signing their name in front of someone and fearing that their hands may tremble is the source of deep embarrassment. Public speaking is a fear beyond words and has social phobics shaking in their boots.

It's been estimated that approximately 35 percent of the population experience some form of a social phobia. If you happen to be one of them, realize that you're not alone. Many people share your fears.

Social fears and phobias can be quite restricting and unfortunately have a way of affecting one's entire lifestyle. Since social phobics have to interact with people all the time, they constantly feel "on display." If their jobs don't require them to give speeches or presentations, then having a public-speaking anxiety probably doesn't seriously affect them. They can work on committees to get things done, just as long as they don't have to announce the findings publicly. But if part of their responsibilities is to give presentations regularly, and they are scared stiff about doing this, then it's a real problem and can influence their choice of jobs and advancement for career opportunities.

Frances works for an up-and-coming computer company. She has just been told by her boss that he's considering recommending her for a new position. It would pay considerably more money, and carry with it more prestige and a large expense account.

Frances was ecstatic. That is, until she was told that part of her job was to give sales presentations at least once a month. She had always feared speaking in public, and even in college she rarely volunteered to speak in class. On the few occasions when she did, she felt a lot of anxiety, her mind went blank, and she could hear her words barely squeaking out.

Hearing about the presentation responsibility put a tremendous burden on Frances. She began obsessing about talking in front of others and looking foolish. She could visualize in her mind what a nervous wreck she'd look like and began hating the upcoming promotion. She started scouting the want ads for other positions, in the hope that she could avoid a catastrophe. Finally she decided it would be best to make a lateral move to another company rather than deal with the anxiety of the new position. Unfortunately for Frances, she let the phobia get the better of her and ruin the chance for a great promotion.

If you can relate to this, then possibly you're also letting your fears and phobias dominate and restrict your opportunities for growth and change.

Paul, an executive for an electronics firm, felt anxious at even the thought of entering a restaurant. The fear started a year and a half before when he was attending an important luncheon meeting and he suddenly felt sick and thought he was going to vomit.

The reality was that he was coming down with a twenty-four-hour virus, but facts are not relevent in phobic thinking. The fear that he could have vomited in a public place preoccupied his thinking. The thought that it *might* happen, the mere association of restaurants and vomiting, made him want to avoid such situations in the future. He soon began to refuse to eat out with his wife, making vague excuses, and she became increasingly angry and frustrated. She started to lose patience with his fear, and they had a lot of arguments around that subject.

Yet restaurants really couldn't be avoided, since part of Paul's work required him to meet clients over business lunches and socialize after hours. He dreaded the experience and obsessed about it beforehand. Those times were torture for him as he continually fretted about "what if" scenarios. As soon as he arrived at a restaurant he'd make a mad dash for the bar, hoping that a drink would settle his anxiety. He'd survey the exits and find out where the bathrooms were, "just in case." He felt dizzy and his heart would skip a beat. He would make excuses for leaving early, feigning other appointments, and felt enormous relief when he got out into the fresh air.

The problem with many phobic people is that they never recognize the following:

1. They are suffering from the fear response.
2. Help is available to conquer the fear.
3. It is possible to live a life free from such fears and phobias.

As I've said before, such fears and phobias are among the most treatable of all problems. So why opt to continue to suffer the pain of anxiety and fear when there are proven, constructive ways of learning to overcome those feelings?

A real problem among social phobics is the fear that other people will discover their anxiety. If this happens they are certain they will be humiliated, and be judged harshly by others. So they avoid parties, public speaking, or any situations where others may judge them.

If you are among the millions who dread social situations and continually make excuses, then it's time to take action. If you reguarly count the number of people in the world who sign credit cards, checks, and contracts, or who pick up a glass of orange juice as if it were nothing, then you are constantly evaluating and berating yourself. Meanwhile you're living with the fear that your anxiety shouts to the world that you're anxious and vulnerable at times.

You may also get scared to expose yourself to the attacks of a hostile person. They could say, "Is anything wrong? You look so tense. Are you always this nervous?"

These remarks are often intended as attacks by angry

and hostile people who are looking for a victim. They are unhappy and envious, so by calling attention to your vulnerabilities, they feel better. People like this are not interested in being sympathetic, but in being agressive. They seize upon the anxiety of others to avoid looking at their own miserable lives.

Alice, a high-school guidance counselor, entered treatment because her signing phobia had increased in intensity. It had started four years before when she was asked by a hostile clerk to present "what felt like fifty forms of identification" in order to verify and approve the check she wrote. She began worrying that maybe her signature wasn't exactly the same on each card, and that the store would not approve her credit. She felt so humiliated by this thought she wanted to run out of the store, and wished she'd never thought of buying the item. In actuality he was only asking for the required two additional forms of identification, but his attitude was condescending and intimidated Alice.

For a while this incident was associated only with signing checks. Yet soon the phobia extended to credit cards and finally affected Alice any time she was asked to sign her name, even in the privacy of her home.

Alice started carrying large sums of cash around with her just to avoid situations in which the possibility of signing her name might arise. She had to gradually learn, however, that trembling hands are hardly a sin! They say nothing about her personally, since the truth of the matter is that she is really a fine, intelligent person with a good marriage, successful career, and lots of close friends.

I felt that group therapy would help her begin to realize that she could be respected and cared for, phobia and all! At some point in group Alice was encouraged by the other members to try to sign in front of them. Because the group was a loving, supportive network, Alice was eventually able to sign (initially only her first name). However, she soon worked up to her address and telephone number, and eventually wrote a brief letter to the group—in group! She was pleased at her progress, yet still hesitant to sign "publicly."

The next task for Alice was to risk writing outside the group. She was encouraged to buy merchandise from a salesperson who was friendly and not intimidating. Although she felt enormous trepidation Alice decided that it was time to try. She looked for and found a congenial saleswoman in a big department store who was helpful to her in selecting a dress. The woman was warm and motherly and had a nice smile, so Alice felt comforted and somewhat relaxed. While in the dressing room she toyed with the idea of paying for the dress with cash. But she immediately thought of the group and myself cheering her on to victory. Alice then signed her first check in four years at that store, "trembling hands and all!"

She felt triumphant and tremendously elated. She told the group what she accomplished and they all were delighted for her. They gave her a strong positive response and Alice felt confident that she was now able to overcome a fear that restricted her for years. She is an example of a determined woman who refused to let her phobias continue to control her behavior.

It's amazing how much energy you can discover within yourself when you work through a phobia! Instead of focusing in on what you can't do, you begin to see possibilities for growth and change in many aspects of your life. It's also better for you to give up on wanting everyone's approval and begin to accept and love yourself, whether you feel anxious or not.

The problem with many fearful people is that they don't actually identify themselves as being phobic at all! They may just take for granted that they feel tense and nervous whenever they have to speak out in class, or go to a restaurant. It's actually somewhat comforting to admit to yourself (and sometimes to others) that the anxiety is quite intense and more than just simple "nerves." Unfortunately, many physicians and even clinicians don't take the time to explain what is happening. (It may be that the "professionals" don't conceptualize and understand fears and phobias themselves. Thus they can't explain it to you.)

By identifying that you have a social phobia you can begin to take the steps necessary to conquer the fear. As I've said before: *Phobias are among the most treatable of all problems!* If you think about it this way, then why not opt to start working through your anxiety and fear and free yourself from its constraints?

Social phobics are scared to let someone else see their vulnerabilities. They imagine that people will take jabs at them behind their back, and also they feel foolish themselves for acting (in their minds) so stupidly. If you have a fear of performing in public, you're constantly obsessed with how smooth other people are when they're on stage, and what a quivering piece of jelly you are when you stand in front of the audience.

Or, you may live in constant fear that you'll be detected by someone critical who will focus attention on your quietness or your hesitation as you try to speak at a meeting.

The problem for many social phobics is that they use the typical defense of avoidance. They refuse to go to restaurants, cancel interviews, and stay far away from a job that requires oral presentations.

Public speaking can create an anxiety so primitive that it strikes terror into the heart of the most courageous. In a recent survey, public speaking ranked ahead of dying as the number one fear of many people.

Terri belonged to a society of professional business-women. One day she was asked by the president of her chapter to speak at an upcoming meeting about the problems of being a woman in a conservative banking corporation that is 95 percent male. Terri was great at informal meetings on her job, and felt at ease at committee meetings for the society. She had a reputation for speaking her mind clearly and logically. Yet something so formal and important as this talk became horribly scary. She tried desperately to see the inconsistencies of the situation. After all, she made reports to other managers and to her supervisor constantly. Yet somehow this talk seemed in a different class. She tried thinking of the other women in the society whom she liked, yet this didn't help. All she could imagine was how she would make a blundering fool of herself and be drummed out of the organization as a phony.

That's precisely why social fears cause such psychic pain. Fearful people are continually surveying people's reactions to them, feeling that their anxieties are in plain view. For some a mere cough signals a possible gag response, and vomiting will surely follow. The button to be pushed is individual and depends upon your fear response.

Bruce was continually worrying about whether the

zipper on his pants was open. After urinating, he would obsessively check and recheck that it was up. The fantasy of being humiliated went back to an actual experience he had in fourth grade, in which his other classmates teased him for forgetting to zip up his fly. Bruce's mind was more on the status of his zipper than it was on connecting with the people around him. To some, he seemed aloof, which was not at all his personality.

Judy continually worried about falling down in public, or, worse yet, fainting. This particular fear intensified when she was invited to a party and an attractive man asked her to dance. She didn't want to look like a fool in front of everyone. She imagined people calling for an ambulance because she fainted. The fear became so strong that she started to decline dances, and, unfortunately, this fear spread to avoiding parties altogether.

Such nightmares are enough to make anyone of us afraid to socialize, go to a shopping mall, or even fantasize about writing in public.

If you can relate to this, you're probably a great observer of all the people in the world who regularly speak out in public, look forward to parties, and feel comfortable in restaurants. Meanwhile you hate interviews with a passion, and hardly feel excited about the challenge of working with a new director.

Instead of continuing to avoid situations that trigger those frightening feelings, you'll need to face your fears. In this way you can begin to still the negative voice that tells you you can't sign your name with someone looking on, or that you'll faint if you try to speak at a meeting.

You may find it incomprehensible at this point to

even imagine feeling comfortable in a restaurant and actually enjoying your meal. You'll need to start to explore new, alternative ways of dealing with your fears, and not let them get the better of you. I know it's terribly hard when you have such a dread of something, but there are constructive methods that I am going to show you so that you can overcome this anxiety.

Social phobias cause you to constrict your activities, relationships, and career. But as you begin to come to terms with your anxiety, you'll dread these situations less and less. In fact, you'll start seeing them as another situation that challenges you to use your newfound positive energy. As your image of yourself strengthens, then the fears of what others think will lessen. You'll begin to care more about yourself than how others see you. Their views will be interesting but not relevant to how you feel about yourself. This will come as a direct result of believing in yourself, and of loving and supporting yourself. That is my goal for you and one that, together, we are going to achieve.

CHAPTER EIGHT

AGORAPHOBIA: THE FEAR OF THE FEELINGS

> Nothing is so much to be feared as fear.
> —Henry David Thoreau

AGORAPHOBIA. Even the name sounds scary. In actuality it affects an estimated 10 to 20 million Americans, so it's hardly uncommon, although its sufferers feel their problems and symptoms are unique. Agoraphobia does, however, differ from both social and simple fears in some very distinct ways. It isn't necessarily restricted to a specific object like a plane, escalator, or animal. Nor does it seem to limit itself to particular social events, such as going to restaurants, speaking in public, signing checks, or avoiding parties. Instead agoraphobia seems to affect the entire being of the sufferer and causes torturous anxiety at what seems to be every turn.

What exactly is agoraphobia? The essential symptoms experienced during an attack are palpitations, choking or smothering sensations, dizziness, sweating, faintness, trembling, fear of dying or going crazy, and the development of an anticipatory fear of such feelings.[1]

With agoraphobics, the fear of the panicky feelings arises as soon as they open their eyes, and is intense enough to cause them to think twice about getting out of bed. What makes their anxiety so intense is the elusiveness of the fear, the feeling that anything will bring on an anxiety attack. Sometimes it seems as though they've no reprieve from its clutches. Minute after minute will be another battle with the feelings of panic that may seize them unexpectedly. The doorbell rings, and there's parcel post expecting them to answer. Now they've got to "act" sane and not be terrified for the few minutes while they sign for the package.

Terror is the key word here. It is unlike the feelings that other fearful people experience. It is overwhelmingly intense, and seems to come *without warning*. It is not restricted to particular places or things. It is probably one of the worst experiences that anyone in their wildest imagination could fathom. It comes as a bolt out of the blue, and can cause its victims to feel temporarily disoriented and confused. They tremble from fright, perspire, and experience a rapid heartbeat, perhaps even rubbery knees and assorted other symptoms. And since the panic associated with agoraphobia is unexpected, the fear of these panic attacks arises anywhere and everywhere. The only escape from these awful feelings is to be either in the company of a safe person, such as a spouse, relative, or friend, or within a safety zone. This zone could include one's neighborhood or certain stores. For some, the safety zone is restricted to within the confines of their home or apartment where they can avoid the outside world completely.

Agoraphobia usually begins in a person's twenties and starts rather unexpectedly. The first panic attack is something that sufferers can recount in precise detail years later, because of the intensity of the attack. The experience is so traumatic that it causes its victim to recoil with terror. "Am I losing my mind?" "Am I having a heart attack?"

This terror is something only the agoraphobic can understand. Seemingly simple tasks, like shopping, standing in a bank line, even answering the phone, can become Herculean challenges. For many agoraphobics such everyday tasks defeat them, and instead they retreat to the safety of their homes. Sometimes they quit their jobs, retreat from friends, and become virtual prisoners of fear.

There are many theories about why someone becomes agoraphobic. There is also a lot of research on the subject. Yet for the present, if you suffer from agoraphobia, you know only too well how your symptoms plague you and dominate your thinking without reading a word of research.

Gloria, a forty-year-old free-lance writer, can remember vividly when she had her first panic attack. She was asked to be the guest lecturer at her alma mater after selling her second book. She rehearsed what she would say and was more than prepared for her topic. What she wasn't prepared for was the panic attack that hit her. A former senior professor who was jealous and competitive with Gloria when she was a student began baiting her hostilely in the question and answer period. She could feel herself getting more and more anxious, but managed to get through the lecture, gripping the podium for dear life. Afterward, the hostile professor came up to her, and as he started to speak, she panicked again. Her body seemed to shake uncontrollably and her mind went blank. She managed to eke out some words and then fled to the safety of the restroom, asking herself, "Oh my God, what happened to me?" She stayed there until the panic subsided.

But it returned a month later when Gloria was invited to give a lecture at another college. She tried desperately to get through her talk, but panic hit once more. After the lecture she raced home. Soon the fear cycle spiraled. She began to make excuses to her husband for not going out: "I've been so busy writing that I couldn't get to the bank." Actually she knew she was petrified of feeling anxious while standing in line. Her friends invited her out to lunch, but she declined, saying, "I'd love to, but I'm dieting." Soon, she dreaded going to the supermarket or the library or getting stuck in traffic because tremendous panic fears could arise. Although Gloria continued to write, her world became smaller and more restrictive.

Soon Gloria dreaded having an entire day before her. As soon as she got out of bed she began to worry that a panic spasm would hit her. Her fear of the anxiety was intensified by thinking of all the things she had to do during the day. She was scared stiff of driving on the highway, having a panic attack before her publisher, and generally feeling vulnerable and exposed, even to her closest friends.

Gloria's first thoughts for the day all were focused on the "worst that could happen." Her thoughts were all catastrophic in nature. Instead of being able to picture herself as a highly talented woman, conscientious and dedicated to her work, she saw herself as a small child in desperate need of protection. This is a common belief among agoraphobics, who see themselves as weak, helpless, and vulnerable.

If you are agoraphobic, you know what that feels like. You take your dog with you in the hope that you might not feel all alone. You wear certain clothes that might protect you, since the last time you wore that outfit, panic didn't strike. Finally you decide that just leaving the house will bring on the panic, so you're better off staying home. Anything to avoid those terrible feelings. But you pay a high price, which is why I want to help you overcome these fears.

I am going to help you to reorganize your imagined belief that imminent disaster lurks around every corner, and begin to help you believe more in yourself and your talents and abilities. I want to separate you from your panic and show you that the key to success is within yourself. I'm going to show you how to unlock your potential and quiet your panic.

Mary, a twenty-five-year-old law student with exceptional abilities, had her first panic attack as she attempted to give a presentation in front of her class, during her third semester at school. Prior to this she had an excellent grade-point average and enjoyed her classwork immensely.

Mary's panic attack consisted of her mind going temporarily blank, her mouth becoming dry, and her heart pounding furiously. Her hands trembled so much that she couldn't write and her legs felt weak. All she could think of was getting out of there as soon as possible. After the panic experience she attempted to avoid courses that would require class participation (which was impossible), and started to dread classes, while berating herself for even beginning law school in the first place.

It's important to examine, but not dwell on, the first panic attack. This way you can begin to understand some of the dynamics of what occurred, and thus give the "first panic" less importance than it deserves.

With Mary it became clear that she was threatened by a member of the class who appeared to be arrogant and hostile. She expected that she would be attacked for her ideas and look foolish before the class and the professor. So instead, her mind turned against itself and thus Mary "attacked" herself through panic and anxiety.

This experience with panic didn't stop here. After awhile she began to have panic attacks when standing in line at the store, driving to shopping malls, and ultimately just seeing a neighbor. The panic seemed to follow her everywhere. She started to feel trapped in the confines of an anxious body and mind.

Fortunately for Mary, she confided in Jean, a good friend who was vaguely aware of her situation. Jean realized that Mary was restricting her life more and more and encouraged her to seek professional help. She knew Mary's strengths and was confident that with help Mary could deal successfully with the panic.

At this point Mary admitted that her fears were getting the best of her, and agreed that she needed some outside help. Motivation has a lot to do with curing the fear response! Despite her anxiety about seeking professional help she was determined to conquer these fears and get on with her aspirations and dreams.

During individual treatment we explored ways for her to begin to tolerate manageable levels of anxiety so that she could resume her activities, despite her fear of the panic.

Mary was able to graduate law school (with honors!) and moved on to a successful career as an attorney. She's a great example of how confronting the fear response can free you from the clutches of the panicky feelings. Instead of continually being victimized by fears, you can start seeing yourself as capable of pushing through these terrors, and getting on with your life!

Many agoraphobics take their behavior seriously. Even showing up at the shopping mall requires them to be at and look their very best. If they are in a store, they feel obligated to buy something, or else they feel they'll look stupid. They give enormous power to others to judge them, making them feel powerless and inadequate.

Agoraphobics set difficult standards for themselves. They give too much importance to their appearance and demand of themselves that they not tremble, their heart not pound, or that their knees not become rubbery. In addition, like other phobics, they worry that someone might recognize their anxiety and make a hostile comment about it. In the scheme of things who really cares whether someone notices? The person next to you in the checkout line is probably more concerned about how long the line will take, and oblivious to whether your knees wobble or not. Yet to the agoraphobic every experience becomes another situation that potentially spells disaster. This is where we have to focus on helping you to care less about how you look or feel if a panic spasm strikes.

What if you're in the supermarket reading your list as usual, and suddenly someone from high school that you hadn't seen for ten years appears? All of a sudden you experience instant panic. You want to run, can't think for a moment, and clutch your grocery cart for dear life. You want to escape and get out of there as fast as your legs can carry you. One minute you seem fine—the next minute terrorized! Is it any wonder why a person would do anything to avoid feeling victimized by those intense feelings? When a person can feel okay one minute and frantic the next, the experience becomes overwhelming. This is the crux of agoraphobia . . . the gigantic surge of panic and the ongoing fear of panic.

Agoraphobia was once thought to be associated with women and more specifically with housewives in particular; indeed, it was known as the "housewives' syndrome." It's now known that many of the sufferers are also men, who sometimes have the courage to admit to their fears without imagining themselves as unmasculine and weak. Ideas of masculinity and femininity have nothing whatsoever to do with the fear response, but they do change your image of yourself and leave you, male or female, with a bruised ego.

This is precisely why my program includes heightening your self-esteem, while working on the anxiety response. The more you care about yourself and focus less on the fears, the more your phobia will take a back seat.

Agoraphobics typically evaluate themselves by the physical sensations that accompany panic. If they had a good day and managed to get through it without panic, they may experience a glimmer of hope. Yet all the while they're still feeling that tomorrow will probably bring a turn for the worse, and that they'll be right back where they started.

You may be so accustomed to guilt, anxiety, and accompanying worthless feelings that you experience them as a part of your thoughts about yourself, and take them for granted.

You are not your panic, your fears of leaving the house, driving, or speaking out! You are a sensitive, creative person whose fears dominate you at this point in time.

There's so much more to you than your symptoms, since they're merely a part of you and hardly the total you. Your sensitivity and awareness of others are incredibly more valued traits than judging yourself by your anxiety. Whether you have anxiety or not is irrelevant to your strong character. This is why as I show you how to feel more confident about yourself, you'll be less likely to be thrown by anxiety, or by people who seem to enjoy either making you unduly anxious or calling attention to your anxiety symptoms.

In succeeding chapters I am going to show you how to feel less vulnerable if someone tells you you're looking tense, or asks why you're so nervous. Unfortunately many agoraphobics feel devastated by the question and fumble for an explanation.

It's important not to believe that your goals are at a

permanent standstill and that you have nothing to look forward to but a life filled with fear, anxiety, and panic responses. Imagine, just for one moment, how wonderful it would be to be rid of all the fear that you experience day by day?

I want you to realize that that awful, vulnerable feeling that grips you when you first wake up, and may even stay with you throughout the day, can eventually be quieted. You too, as so many before you, can learn to look forward to the day ahead without expecting or experiencing panic and terror. I would like you to think of myself as being there with you. Think of me as someone who wants phobic people to become all they are capable of being. Together we will take the first tentative steps toward confronting your agoraphobia.

Many agoraphobics feel that they are not understood and feel different from others. They also feel tremendously alone. Each time you think or feel this way, I want you to take comfort in the fact that you have a huge protective family of fearful people. Many have been able to conquer their symptoms, while others are still struggling with them. Isn't it time to join hands with such a large extended family and wish each other well? The positive energy that can come from knowing you're not alone in your struggle can be quite exhilarating. You are not waging a private battle; many others feel the same way you do.

Try to imagine yourself living a life without the fear of anxiety! You can begin to use your creative energies and talents to overcome both the fear of the internal sensations of panic, and the external use of avoidance, to challenge your agoraphobia.

Just as with anything, you'll need to practice in order

to diminish the power of fear. If you practice getting out, even if it means exchanging a few words with a neighbor or store clerk, that's the road to success. The reason is simple: avoidance reinforces fear. On the other hand, each effort to overcome fear strengthens you to move closer to final victory. That is the purpose of this book and my goal for you.

CHAPTER NINE

BATTLING FEARS
OF SUCCESS

> Success is a journey, and not a destination.
> —Ben Sweetland

WHY in God's name would anyone have a fear of success? You can understand a fear of driving or flying or public speaking or the dentist. You can even understand why some would ruminate obsessively about their health. Yet fear of success may seem strange, almost unbelievable, unless of course, you've wondered if you're more ambivalent about achievement than perhaps you care to admit.

Success fears are frequently elusive, and they're never quite as easy to recognize as most other kinds of fears. However they are quite common and we hear about their consequences all the time. Their chief symptom is self-defeating behavior; the person who fears success has various ways to avoid it. Some people, for instance, whine about the dearth of eligible mates. Then they finally meet the kind of person they've been describing as perfect, but on the very first date, act sarcastic and critical. They go home knowing that they'll never see this person again, and wonder why they've acted so stupidly. Or worse yet, they think they were clever and witty and can't understand why they never hear from the person. And there are others who, after waiting months for a certain kind of job, arrive late for the interview and destroy their chances before they start.

How often do we hear about sports figures who are suspended from playing because of drugs? Or rock and movie stars who overdose at the heights of their careers? Or the politician who took a bribe, and for a mere pittance destroyed his career? It seems that for many people, enjoying success is not in the cards.

Judging by their earlier actions, you might speculate that all these people were motivated to succeed. Yet what happened? What makes people blow chances that could earn them a place at the pinnacle of success? And what about those just beginning relationships and careers who throw a monkey wrench into the machinery?

Why do people do this? The answer quite simply is a self-destructive urge that screams, "Don't succeed! Or if you dare to, crush yourself now!" Some are afraid of surpassing the accomplishment of a parent, who was jealous and competitive with the child. "Who do you think you are having boyfriends at your age?" continually asked a divorced mother of her seventeen-year-old daughter. The girl got the idea early that she wasn't supposed to succeed in love, because her mother had failed. She sabotaged relationships with boys so as not to lose her mother's "love," which took precedence over everything.

Too often an envious parent plays dirty like this. You may be putting yourself through college while your parents are high school dropouts, who constantly urge you to "get a job and earn some decent money." Instead of encouraging you and helping you to select courses that are right for you, they send a clear message: "I didn't, and by God you're not going to."

Beth, a mother of two young children, wanted to continue her education. When she finally was able to take a course at night at the local college, her mother was critical. "How could you be a good mother and leave your children, just to take a course?"

To buck this tide requires a lot of determination and self-discipline, not to mention self-love. For many of us, getting parental approval has been an ongoing quest started in childhood that stays with us even as adults.

Another reason for the fear of success is the anticipation that people in our lives will resent or reject us. As we do better in the world, we run the danger of losing their support and risking their anger. Alice, for example, would regularly meet for lunch and dinner with two close friends, Marianne and Joyce. Often the conversation would turn to their relationships with men. All three women concurred that many of the men they met were cold and unfeeling. Each of these women had suffered disappointments and had turned to one another for reassurance. Especially when a relationship was going badly, these women would seek solace and advice from each other.

Finally Alice met a man, Fred, a junior architect, who

seemed interested in many of the things that Alice enjoyed, and was truly compassionate. They had met at a health club and struck up a conversation. Alice mentioned that she was in the process of redoing her apartment and Fred took a real interest; he came in the next week with a list of designs culled from magazines.

Alice and Fred started going out together a few times a week for a month, and had just slept together for the first time. She wondered if she was falling in love with him, and talked about him to her friends. To her surprise, they were unenthusiastic. It wasn't that they put Fred down; in fact, Marianne, said, "He sounds nice," but then abruptly changed the subject. After awhile Alice felt a growing sense of discomfort if she even mentioned Fred's name. Marianne and Joyce would give each other looks of boredom and annoyance, so that after awhile Alice stopped talking about him altogether. Eventually as Alice and Fred's relationship prospered, Marianne and Joyce stopped calling.

There are many reasons people don't want to succeed. Besides being petrified of surpassing a parent or being afraid of someone's jealousy, they may simply be scared of exhibiting themselves as an assertive person. If you suspect that you may consciously or unconsciously fear being successful, whether in relationships or on the job, then it's essential to start identifying your fears so that you don't defeat yourself.

Tracy, a talented off-Broadway actress in her late twenties, always stayed up late the night before an audition and showed up late. She then continually complained about not getting parts, but she sabotaged herself before she got started.

Sometimes stage fright is a way performers have of

hindering themselves. The inner voice says, "I'm petrified of singing tomorrow. I know my throat will close up and I'll start shaking." Or, "I'll forget my lines and look like a fool." It's important to investigate another line of thought: "What if I did get the part?" Perhaps underlying the stage fright is the *real* fear, a primitive dread of success.

Situations like this happen frequently. People say one thing and yet their behavior proves them different. "I really want that raise," someone might say. Yet that person is always late for work and has been spoken to by his boss about the tardiness.

Sometimes a phobia may develop because of success fears. Phil, a computer programmer for a large airline, recently received a transfer to the head office. Along with the transfer went a large jump in salary and a management position. He was thrilled! The first week was exciting. Being gregarious he enjoyed meeting new people. On Monday of his second week however, he suddenly had an anxiety attack on the elevator. He was scared out of his mind. He began shaking and his knees turned to jelly. He thought he was having a heart attack. After this experience he went straight to the doctor and was given a prescription for tranquilizers. For six months he regularly took the medication before work, before lunch, and just before getting on the elevator at the end of the day. Phil was worried that he would become dependent on the medication, but he couldn't even approach the elevator without taking the tranquilizer. It was at this point that his wife urged him to get some professional help and he was referred to me.

When I first saw Phil he was feeling depressed and helpless and was seriously contemplating leaving his position. It would have been terrible to act on such feelings. Not only would Phil have left an excellent job, with fantastic benefits, but also he would have set up an avoidance pattern that's hard to break. The anxiety would have then ruled his life and controlled his actions.

First, Phil needed to slowly decrease the tranquilizers, under the supervision of a physician. Afterward, he gradually had to learn to face the feared object, the elevator, and diminish the power of the fear response. This was accomplished within a few months and Phil felt terrific. He was now tranquilizer-free, although he did carry the medication around with him "just in case."

Phil was satisfied with the results, yet had a desire to understand how the fear happened to him in the first place. Careful analysis indicated that underneath the symptom was a powerful unconscious dread of success. He had a kind of love-hate relationship with success: he wanted it desperately but feared it equally as much. Phil was afraid of becoming more successful than his father, who was a supervisor for a small electronics firm. The closer that Phil came to surpassing his father the more anxiety he felt. The conflict led him to put his success on hold and thus he tried to defeat himself through fear. Once he realized this, his phobia was no longer necessary, and he began to enjoy reaping the rewards of his success. He started to take advantage of the flight benefits his company offered, and he and his wife began to travel extensively.

Success fears are one of the few areas where I find it necessary to have a deeper understanding of the cause, since you don't want the symptoms to show up elsewhere. Phil easily could have stopped treatment after a few months, once he was no longer dependent on tranquilizers, but he wanted to get a handle on his unconscious motivations. As a result of his desire to explore himself analytically, he was able to identify other areas that were keeping him from enjoying himself.

Self-defeating persons are usually extremely transparent to everyone except themselves. They constantly deny that their behavior is destructive. The researcher who falsifies data or the person caught shoplifting while carrying large sums of money is each bent on destroying a career and a life. Yet more subtle are those who also fear success but have more covert ways of putting obstacles in their paths. Not handing in assignments on time, tardiness, or not paying bills when they are due are other examples. Alcohol and drug abuse, compulsive eating, and gambling are glaring examples of self-defeating behavior that not only interferes with success but destroys people's lives.

People who suddenly develop a fear of driving after landing a great position that requires the use of a car, or find themselves unable to board a plane after receiving a promotion that requires them to fly abroad, also show symptoms of the fear of success.

If you find that any of these examples relates to you, then you'll need to investigate your success fears to avoid being a target for self-destruction.

Success is the reward that comes from hard work and discipline. It's important to appreciate yourself and your accomplishments and keep to a minimum anything that might threaten your achievements. Drug and alcohol abuse have destroyed many promising careers and should be considered a potential enemy to success. If you find yourself relying on drugs in order to feel something, or if you realize that you're more subtly subverting possible opportunities for yourself, it's time to get some help.

When you've worked hard to get somewhere, you need to appreciate the rewards. That's why it is essential to work for and not against yourself. Indeed, I want you to recognize that you, more than anyone else, need to feel good about your triumphs.

CHAPTER TEN

DO I NEED TO EXPLORE THE UNCONSCIOUS MEANINGS OF MY SYMPTOMS?

DISCOVERING the unconscious meaning of any symptom can be exciting. Realizing why you must have a clear desk surface at all times, or why you refuse to travel on the thirteenth day of each month, is enlightening, and can sometimes lead to changes in your behavior. It may give you more freedom to choose what you want, and not be restricted by compulsiveness or superstition. It's always interesting to learn why you fear heights or get anxious in a crowded room, or why you obsess about your health. Any insight correctly interpreted by a therapist can satisfy that emotional and intellectual curiosity. Finding out why you fear an ongoing commitment to a relationship can have a large impact on your life.

There is considerable pleasure derived from being able to connect your fear response to its early roots that can certainly be enriching, and give you a sense of yourself as an individual with a particular history.

This is just fine, if you decide to pursue analysis for that reason. Some people do, and find such insights useful. They love to chatter at parties about what early traumas they suffered and hook this up to why they can't have a decent relationship today.

During the last twenty years, fears and phobias have been studied extensively, and evidence has shown us that the value of analytic insight in treating these problems, however, has been greatly overestimated. This is especially true when it comes to the fear response. Psychoanalysis, which equates insight with cure, has been a great disappointment to many phobic sufferers. Just talk to the millions of phobics who have either made no progress or actually have gotten worse through the psychoanalytic method.

In the past psychoanalytically oriented therapists spent many years analyzing phobic people without ever helping them overcome the crippling social consequences of their fears or phobia. Despite this remarkable lack of success, many of these therapists still persist in working with a method which gets their patients nowhere except to the therapist's office.[1]

For wasted years many phobics dutifully lay on the couch and free associated to their dreams and past memories. The analyst would mutter a few interpretations as if his or her words were magical incantations, designed to make the patient's fears vanish instantaneously. Alas and alack, they never did. These patients left the analyst's office feeling just as frightened as when they walked in fifty minutes before, or five years before. As a matter of fact analysis may actually delay a fearful person's progress by concentrating on the past rather than confronting the present fear.

Phobic people tend to be perfectionists, so naturally to please the analyst and get his or her approval, they concentrate hard on the origins of their fears. They dutifully remember their dreams and pay for their sessions on time. Unfortunately, the price many fearful and phobic people pay is that while they are busy pleasing the analyst by being a "good patient," they are also suffering miserably at the hands of the fear response. Day after day they may ruminate about how they can't enter the subway for fear of suffocating. Then they tell themselves, "I have to remember that this is because my sister put that blanket over my head when I was five. I'll have to tell my analyst this." The evidence says that such memories are useless in removing fears. "Most phobic people have not been relieved of their symptoms when they were able to understand the displacement of their fears."[2] It appears that only in the area surrounding success phobias can analytic knowledge of the origin of these fears lead to behavioral change.

Pamela, a bright, vivacious woman in her late twenties, had an extremely punitive background. Her parents, particularly her mother, was harsh to the point of being abusive. Her father was absent most of the time on business, so that Pamela got the brunt of her mother's aggression and anger.

As a child Pamela was punished by being locked out of the house if she was five minutes late coming home from the playground. Pamela would pound on the door and plead to be let in, but to no avail. Her brother, who was four years older, would be left in charge of Pamela when their parents went out and would frequently lock her inside a closet when they were gone.

As Pamela reached her mid-twenties, she developed panic attacks associated with buses, planes, subways, even cars—any place she felt trapped. She had an impulse to run and scream and experienced claustrophobic feelings.

She went to an analyst affiliated with a training institute, and started seeing him twice a week. (Classical analysis is in fact three times a week. However, such methods are rarely used today. Instead, analytic theory is adapted to much less frequent sessions.) He took notes, said very little, and wanted her to recall her dreams and early memories. Pamela went to him for five years and had a lot of intellectual insight into her past. The problem was that Pamela's fears worsened. During this time, she began to dread even leaving the house.

In this case knowing the unconscious message was not helpful. Pamela would have benefited more from consulting someone who helped her tolerate the feelings of fear. Although concentrating on the early origins of her fears expressed by her dreams and free associations was interesting, it was not very useful. Even Freud believed that direct confrontation with the phobic situation itself is essential for recovery. He stated: "One succeeds only when one can induce them . . . to struggle with the anxiety while they make the attempt."[3]

In other words, the only way to overcome anxiety is to experience the fear when it arises, and not merely discuss the origins of it. If you continue to avoid the fearful situation, you have no chance of success. The problem with the analytic method applied to fears and anxieties is that it encourages a passivity to present day reality. To have the analyst interpret "separation anxiety," for example, as stemming from early traumas only keeps the patient rooted in the past. Such information isn't worth a damn when you're in the grip of the fear response.

Let's look at a person with a fear of public speaking. Faced with a podium, analytic knowledge in no way diminishes the anxiety. To know that public speaking stirs up fears of "exhibitionism" or possible "attacks by authority figures" isn't going to ease the symptoms of a person with a pounding heart, dry mouth, and rubbery knees. It's not enough to have interpretation made to a fearful person. Instead, observable change takes place when a patient is helped to confront slowly the fearful situation, and not give in to anxiety.

Psychoanalysis has largely ignored the question of what causes observable changes in phobic behavior. It seems necessary now to shift the tension to the phenonema of observable changes in their context to open new and more promising directions for the study and treatment of phobic people.[4]

That is not to say that analysis cannot be effective in the understanding of the overall personality, or the treatment of certain dynamics such as the fear of success, for anxiety about success has some powerful unconscious motivations. If you find yourself doing self-destructive things, perhaps your fear of success is stronger than your desire for it. This being the case, psychoanalytic psychotherapy can be quite useful, since your conscious mind probably isn't aware of the unconscious need to destroy yourself.

The relationship you have with a therapist is terribly important. If you find that you're speaking to a deity who perks up only when you mention dreams or early childhood traumas, it might be a good idea to shop elsewhere. You'll need a warm, supportive person to help you through the rough spots as you begin to take the risks necessary to cure your fear or phobia. Someone whose technique is to be silent and distant, and who measures his or her words as if they were pearls of wisdom, is not the best therapist for fears. To recall how embarrassed you felt giving book reports in the sixth grade in no way lessens your fear of speaking before groups. For fearful people a more interactive relationship is advised.

Fears and phobias are in the *present!* It's true that the cause may directly relate to past feelings and memories, but the reality is that we have to deal with the here and now—to get you to enter the shopping mall, speak in public, or get on the plane or elevator. *All the understanding of what caused you to feel the fear in the first place isn't about to soothe you when you feel panic!*

I recently heard of a psychologist who advised his patient to place a brown paper bag over her head whenever she felt panic. Can you for one moment imagine taking the elevator with your co-workers and suddenly breaking out a paper bag that you put over your head? To say you'd look foolish is an understatement! I can hear your supervisor now: "We wanted to promote you, but, uh . . . about that bag you carry." Or what if you're on a deserted subway in Chicago at night and you put a bag over your head when you feel panicky? To say you are inviting danger is once again an understatment. This same psychologist went on to give even worse advice: the patient was told that she would always suffer from these fears whenever she attempted to do something new and challenging. Panic would always be with her. Not too encouraging, is it? Finally the person was told she was suffering from "separation anxiety," which is a childhood fear of being abandoned (all of this from the first consultation, incidently). Yet, although the basis of panic can in fact be separation anxiety, this knowledge isn't going to soothe her in the midst of an attack. That's why the study of the unconscious is fascinating, yet should not be confused with a cure.

In selecting a therapist who is right for you, you'll need someone who is empathetic and humane, with an emotional as well as intellectual grasp of fears and phobias. If he or she is knowledgeable only through book learning and lacks the qualities necessary to help you change, the therapy will leave you frustrated and feeling hopeless and despairing about your condition.

Keep these points in mind when you select someone to help you through the anxiety maze. You deserve someone who understands and empathizes and is in fact able to help you.

PART TWO

THE PATH AHEAD
TO NO MORE FEARS

IN the last ten chapters I have talked about the fear response. Now you are ready to take active steps to diminish the anxiety and move forward in all directions. I want to outline some principles of action that will show you how to conquer the fear response. You're going to feel wonderful as you see yourself doing things that until recently seemed impossible.

Conquering the fear response is one of the most exhilarating victories any person can achieve. Experiences you never thought conceivable will be yours: going to that company party without the usual jitters or fastening your seatbelt on a plane without the sense of dread. It will be as if you left your fear reactions at home. For the first time, you can become the person you've hoped to be— assertive and self-confident. When you have finished this book, you will feel truly heroic!

You can reach this place by following the principles outlined in the succeeding chapters. Of course, you must proceed step by step, but hard work will produce results. Many things will be possible once you leave the small world in which your fears have enclosed you.

In the meantime, keep the picture of future success as you suffer present fear—it's very important to imagine where you're headed. The time will come when you'll be able to do things without your knees buckling and your hands sweating. You've come a great distance already by acknowledging your fears and deciding to take action against them. That in itself is a crucial step forward. Other steps will include rewriting your old fear script, paying attention to nutrition, exercising, soothing and rewarding yourself, and learning how to deal with hostiles. By doing the above, you can change that inner voice and begin to write a successful script for yourself.

CHAPTER ELEVEN

ACCEPTING THE FEARFUL FEELINGS

NEARLY all children are prone to fear from many sources. You may recall fear of darkness, spiders, thunderstorms, or large dogs. All fears are more acute to the child who feels alone.

How your parents dealt with your fears largely determined how you handled these feelings as a child—and continue to do so as an adult. If they managed to soothe you with kind words, or by holding you, rubbing your forehead, reading a story, or even distracting you, then most probably you suffered less from your fears then and can more easily manage them today. If, however, your parents themselves became anxious, were prone to visible attacks of fear, and didn't comfort you, then you are very likely to feel victimized by fear as an adult.

It's our task now to begin to program you with a different, more accepting voice. Instead of reacting as you did when you were a small child, I want you to enter a new world, one of enhanced self-esteem and new freedom. I want you to appreciate who you are as a person, and even at times enjoy your eccentricity. In a world of "heroes" who are violent, crude, and out of touch with human feelings, how delightful to be sensitive, artistic, and concerned about others. I want you to revel in these qualities instead of asking, "Oh God! What's wrong with me?" I want you to develop your own sense of self without trying to conform to the expectations of everyone else around you. This means accepting both physical and emotional feelings that may be uncomfortable and loving yourself for who you are, fears and all. In short, you need to become a soothing parent to yourself, as a way of overcoming your anxieties and fears.

Together we're going to help you recognize someone else's words of caution as just that . . . someone else's words! The new vocabulary will help you become the soothing parent to yourself who's not afraid to take risks, the comforting parent to yourself that you very much desire. The list that follows is designed to help you in this:

1. When you begin to feel the anxiety soar, speak reassuringly to yourself.

2. Use gentle tones; don't increase the anxiety by attacking yourself for your fears.
3. Imagine yourself being comforted by someone who would accept you, fears and all.
4. Remember that you're not alone in your feelings—everyone suffers from anxiety in one form or another.
5. Think of what you wanted to hear when you felt frightened as a child, and say those things now.

It's not necessary to wonder why you're so much more tense than the next person. Rather, think of how exciting it will be to overcome the anxiety and live a life free from fear! What a wonderful role to begin to accept—that of being a good friend and parent to yourself. After all, who deserves it more?

Sensitive, caring people need some assistance to become all they can be, free from the blocks that anxiety causes. When your mind stops focusing on what you can't do and shifts to what you can do, your energy will be released. You will be able to do new things rather than imagine fearful responses.

Cliff, a successful architect in his early forties, had a tremendous fear of letting people know that he was frightened of heights. His job required him to visit some very tall skyscrapers and draw plans for clients, but he hated every trip up into the dreaded heights. When he had to survey a view from four floors or higher, he would venture toward the window with jelly legs and pounding heart, imagining that he'd leap through the glass. Although he loved his work, he realized that he had begun to avoid prospective clients who required him to be anywhere above his safety zone of the first three floors.

Cliff's wife was also an accomplished architect and she noticed that he was turning down lucrative offers that could have enhanced his career. After confronting Cliff, she realized that he was letting his fears dominate his work and encouraged him to seek professional help. He consulted a local psychiatrist who specialized in drug treatment and was immediately put on an antidepressant. This helped his symptoms, but Cliff and his wife were simply not comfortable with the solution. They feared side effects, and Cliff disliked taking medication in general.

He decided group therapy was a better course of treatment and was fortunate to find a wonderful, supportive group of people that could identify and be sensitive to his problems. Within a few months he was free of his fears and able to tackle some of the biggest skyscrapers in New York, even those with huge plate glass windows!

Cliff's way of conquering the fear was to get in touch with his feelings. But first he had to develop confidence, trust himself, and realize he was hardly a candidate for leaping out of tall buildings. He learned that his fear was irrational and was activated when he felt vulnerable. He began to recognize that his strength was much more powerful than his fear response and that he did not have to "look forward" to a life of medication.

As a result of the support group Cliff was able to accept that he was suffering from the fear response. He resisted the urge to hide his anxiety, which is a critical aspect of overcoming such fears. Remember, the fear response is fueled by avoidance and by hiding. I'm not suggesting that you love your anxiety or tell everyone that you're fearful or phobic, but time and time again I've seen patients improve when they stop trying to hide the fact that they're scared; often with the help of support groups. However, if they fight their anxious and fearful feelings and try to pretend to the outside world that everything's fine and dandy and they're perfectly in control, thank you, they have an additional burden.

Kay was a copy editor for a large newspaper. She found staff meetings torturous, particularly when she had to present her writing in front of the staff. Since these meetings occurred regularly, she lived in constant fear of them. When she walked into the large conference room and took a seat around the long table, her heart started pounding and she felt dizzy. Her inner voice said, "Oh my God, I know I have to speak but I'm terrified someone will see that I'm anxious. I'll look like a fool in front of everyone. Just look at how adult they look and how childish I feel. They're all so much in control of themselves and I must look like a nervous wreck."

The reality was that Kay looked a trifle anxious, but her internal, negative voice made her feel even worse. She was so petrified that someone would attack her for being anxious that she increased the initial fear.

This is how the negativistic thinking styles we learn early in childhood affect our performance today. In Kay's case her father was extremely overprotective and worried obsessively if she was five minutes past her curfew. He always tried to protect her from the "outside world." She learned that her father experienced the world as a place where fear lurked around every corner. Since Kay loved and respected her father, she, too, learned to fear. Because she identified with him, his catastrophic thinking became hers.

Eventually Kay was able to separate her father's fears of dealing with people from her own. She began to adopt her own world view and realized that she could cope with people and criticism much better than she thought.

In quieting the voice that screams "catastrophe!" you must begin to develop the soothing nonanxious voice of the parent who says, "I believe in you and know that you can handle yourself." There's a lot of hostility and many scary things in the world, but when you see yourself as your own soothing parent, the fear response won't be necessary. You'll know you can handle yourself because you'll be tuning into your own talents and strengths, which means accepting all your passionate and intense feelings, including your fears.

In accepting fearful feelings and learning to move past them it's important to remember:

1. If you are with friendly, helpful people you can admit that you suffer from the fear response. Most often people will be sympathetic and share their own experiences with anxiety.

2. When you sense that someone might not understand and will expect you to "get your act together," then naturally you'll have to be on your guard. Here it's essential to accept that you feel fearful and let whatever physical sensations that accompany the fear simply wash over you without monitoring them. Most people haven't the slightest inkling that you're anxious and even if they do, so what? Try to establish a good

screening device if someone points out your anxiety. For example, Margaret had a stuttering problem but she learned that she had ways of dealing with hostile people who pointed it out to her. In the grand scheme, does it really matter? Is Margaret less of a person just because she stutters?

3. By accepting the feelings you're admitting they exist—not pretending you don't have them. As the Eastern martial arts teach us, "Go with the flow of the enemy." To fight and act defensive is to hurt yourself by creating more waves of anxiety.

4. Anxiety, as unpleasant as it is, can be conquered only when you face your fears (even gradually). Try not to run away from situations that evoke fear.

Being able to tolerate the anxiety that gets stirred up when you approach a feared or phobic situation will be enough for you to place a royal feather in your cap. I want you to constantly give yourself credit for doing what you thought impossible just a while ago, as you follow the principles discussed in the succeeding chapters. Even though you may now feel anxious at the thought of going near the shopping mall, you will soon be in your car and on your way. You're going to accept your anxiety and push through it.

You've lived the life of fear long enough. Now it's time to accept yourself and your fears!

CHAPTER TWELVE

SOOTHING YOURSELF

Simple Pleasures are the best refuge of the complex.

—Oscar Wilde

WE all need to be comforted and soothed at times. After a long day of dealing with children or meeting deadlines at the office, what could be more desirable than simply relaxing? Most of us arrive at our own methods for taking a break from daily pressures, so that we can return the next day refreshed and relaxed. Lying on the couch and immersing ourselves in the crossword puzzle, or crocheting, reading, or watching television, are only a few ways we achieve a respite from the tensions of the world.

However, anyone suffering from the fear response must forgo even these short moments of rejuvenation. It becomes difficult to unwind because you're starting from a more anxious state. Stress itself can rob you of the ability to repair yourself properly. You know as well as anyone how crummy you feel after a panic attack, and how you would like to put aside your vigilance and stop worrying about the next. You desperately yearn to soothe yourself—all the more reason why you should identify soothing techniques for replenishment.

Even as a small child you had methods to assuage your fears. Maybe you hugged your favorite stuffed animal, drank a glass of warm milk, or sought cuddling from a parent. Or perhaps your mother read you a favorite story before you went to sleep. Or maybe you played with dolls or soldiers, or invented imaginary companions. Whatever the devices, they made you feel better. But what happened along the way? Why can't you soothe yourself now?

What happened is that you feel more stress. That's why I want to talk about soothing techniques you can incorporate in the here and now to reduce your anxiety and help you derive all the benefits associated with relaxation.

Think about what you already do for yourself, the techniques you now utilize. Do you take hot baths or putter in the garden? Perhaps you read a good book curled up by the fireplace on a chilly day, or plan out your next holiday with the travel books before you. Maybe you prefer cooking a comforting meal or dabbling in oil painting. These tasks may replenish you when you're frazzled and are perfectly suited to your needs.

I've spoken about getting you in touch with your creative energy and potential. What you need most of all in times of stress is to tune into the resources you have at your fingertips. The techniques I am going to tell you about are variations of what is called the "relaxation response" and can lead to a wide range of changes, from lowering blood pressure to alleviating pain to relaxing muscles.[1] Relaxation also wards off serious diseases. A growing amount of evidence suggests that people who are more relaxed are less likely to suffer illnesses.[2] All of these relaxation activities are designed to calm you, and are extensions of the things that make you feel good, warm, and relaxed inside. They need to be a part of your *everyday* rituals, not just methods of coping with specific fears as they arise.

Try to recall a time when you were totally at ease and relaxed. In your mind's eye recapture the scene in vivid detail. Was it a sunny day? Were you sitting on the porch, or in a lounge chair in the yard, or perhaps in a canoe on a quiet lake? Were you lying on a beach, or strolling in a park? Were you by yourself or with someone else?

Actively visualize the scene. Make the details as real and familiar as possible; become as specific as you can. Try to recall everything about the event. What did the wind or sun feel like on your skin? What sounds were in the air? Any particular smells like the ocean air, or perhaps floral scents from a field?

The more you remember about the scene the more soothing the effects will be. Each time you call up that image, with its elaborate sensory details, a feeling of calm will return. Soon you'll have the pleasant associations right at your fingertips. While you visualize the relaxed scene, be aware of your breathing. Take long, slow, deep breaths—what psychologists call "diaphragmatic breathing." This will help to bring oxygen to the brain and dissipate accumulated muscle tension. You will quickly feel more relaxed.

"Visualization is just what it sounds like: visualizing an image or scene to help you relax, to build your energy and confidence, or increase your endurance and strength."[3]

As you visualize, you may wish to make use of one of the many commercial cassette tapes that have calm, subliminal messages to assist you in relaxing. Some offer music designed to give you a sense of inner tranquility. Others have subliminal hypnotic suggestions geared toward relaxation. You may find them helpful in achieving a reprieve from fear and anticipatory dread and moving you into a more peaceful state of mind.

Other relaxation techniques include deep breathing for fifteen minutes a day, or sitting quietly with your eyes closed and mentally repeating a simple word or sound. Or take your own hand and gently touch your other hand. Visualize in your mind how it would feel to be warmly touched by a caring, loving person. Be specific. Think of someone who genuinely loved you and wanted to soothe you when you felt frightened as a child, when you had an impulse to run and hide. Or think of someone now who loves you and wants the very best for you. Maybe you were never fortunate enough to have a parent who did this for you. If you're fearful, possibly your parent is the one who raised you to look at the world through fearful eyes. Since you are experiencing fears today, it's important to conjure up someone in the here and now who wants success for you. I know I certainly would love to see you feel less stress and gain an inner sense of calm and freedom from fear.

Again, let me remind you not to use these techniques just when you are feeling stressed. Use them every day to offset past moments of anxiety and move you into a generally more peaceful state of mind. This way they'll become a daily gift to yourself.

I want you to recognize that you have the power to create your own soothing individual for yourself. In your wonderful imagination there exists a parent or someone like a parent who knows and loves you very much. Eventually, you'll begin to see that the good parent is you. So, go ahead when you are anxious: gently hold your hand and imagine how calming such a person is. You are developing the power of auto-suggestion. You can call upon this person just by thinking of what you need at the moment. You can learn, in time, that this soothing, loving parent to the child in you, is always with you. All you need do is visualize, relax, and practice soothing yourself.

I can't emphasize enough how important soothing is. The techniques I've described will help you to calm yourself when anxiety feelings arise, move toward strengthening yourself for a fearful situation, and, most important, learn how to replenish your energies after the jolt of a fearful experience.

CHAPTER THIRTEEN

REWRITING
THE
OLD SCRIPT

> There is only one corner of the universe that
> you can be certain of improving, and that is
> your own self.
>
> —Aldous Huxley

WE all have mental tape recordings that whirl about in our heads replete with all sorts of messages, some encouraging ("I always knew you could do it.") and some preaching fear ("Watch out!" "Be careful!"). It's natural for these messages to have developed. We began by listening to other people's voices—those of parents and other authority figures—until eventually we made them our own. As children we couldn't rely on ourselves, since we were obviously small, helpless, and dependent on adults to tell us who we were and what the world was like around us. So we absorbed the messages of authority figures like a thirsty sponge. We listened eagerly to what they told us, and their words formed the basis of the beliefs about ourselves.

When a parent, or other adult whom we depended on, warned us that catastrophes were always lurking around the corner, we naturally believed them. Some of their ideas were encouraging and useful, but others were harmful and only caused us to feel scared. The small child in us got frightened and became fixated on disastrous endings.

As adults we need to bring these old voices out into the world of today and analyze them from a grown-up perspective. This means we have to listen very carefully on both conscious and unconscious levels to what we say to ourselves.

To accomplish this we must start identifying the negative thoughts from the past as just that . . . relics of a former time. Remember, these are someone else's stale ideas. What is the message? Who is saying it to you? How old were you when you first heard it? Was the danger real then? Is it real today?

Common to fearful people and phobics is a vocabulary of doom, gloom, and disaster. Future situations are imagined as having horrible outcomes. Such scenarios may include getting up to speak before a group and not being able to say a word. Or, worse yet, fainting. Or running off in sheer panic. The inner voice always speaks of disaster; it starts early and never lets up.

It's time to begin to instruct the inner voice to say something uplifting. I don't want you to think that it's utterly impossible to overcome your fears, but instead to imagine the exuberance you'll feel when you don't let your fears stop you. When you accept your fear you are more than halfway there. It's time to change the "I can't" to an "I'll be frightened, but I'll give it my best shot!"

If you're afraid of driving, maybe all you'll be able to do at first is to get into your car and sit for a few minutes. That's not only okay, it's an accomplishment. Each time you take a step like this, you are diminishing the power of the negative shouts. In essence you are saying, "Hey look! You don't know what you're talking about! Not only did I sit behind the wheel, but next time I may even drive to the corner."

The aim here is to help you rephrase your descriptions of situations. For instance, rather than say you are "caught" in a traffic jam, tell yourself you are merely "delayed." Instead of feeling "trapped" on a subway, remind yourself you have an opportunity to read part of a novel you always wanted to read. This way you'll turn something negative into an opportunity to enjoy yourself, for instance, by listening to cassettes or your favorite radio station.

Changing your language, however, doesn't mean you should bury your negative feelings. You might not like being detained momentarily in a supermarket line, and you should admit your annoyance to yourself. This will work toward reducing the tension. When you acknowledge and verbalize your feelings, you lessen the anxiety.

Tuning into your feelings will also get you refreshed and vitalized since you'll spend less energy denying your feelings. The possibilities are endless: Feeling anxious entering a shopping mall? Focus in on how much you'll enjoy wearing the silk blouse you saw in the catalog. You may even want to treat yourself by having the blouse gift wrapped as an additional reward for entering the store, fear and all.

Let's take an example of someone who has a dread of restaurants but must show up for a business luncheon. He could whip himself up into the fear cycle by imagining himself running to the men's room in terror, having an acute panic attack right at the table. But he could also envision a different scenario, one in which he enjoys his food and is knowledgeable about ordering. In his mind he could scan the menu for his favorite pasta and focus in on the conversation. This imaginative act would not be mere distraction but a conscious effort to accent the positive rather than dwell on thoughts of disaster.

To transform the negative energy into a positive force is hard work. Yet you can take solace in the fact that it is certainly within your reach, and not something achievable by everyone but you. It may seem at times impossible to stop thinking negative thoughts, and in reality, it does take practice. But many fearful people have learned to redirect their ideas. With effort, you will be able to change some of those pessimistic internal messages into affirmative assertions of possibility.

Jeanette, a housewife in her late thirties, suffered for years from multiple fear symptoms. She was a sensitive and caring mother of three children, happily married, who had just enrolled in college at night to further her education. But Jeanette feared going to shopping malls by herself, although she was fine when her husband accompanied her. She dreaded speaking out at PTA meetings and driving on the highways.

I had to show Jeanette how to ignore the inner voice of failure and disaster and replace it with a gentler, soothing one. She began to alter these messages, applying the following principles to rewrite her old script:

1. She became aware of how she was programming herself through her thoughts to experience anxiety.
2. She started to substitute positive ideas for her more catastrophic ones.
3. Instead of believing that she couldn't undertake certain activities, she recognized that she could at least try.
4. She allowed herself the anxiety without adding additional fears. Instead of telling herself, "If I'm on the freeway and I get stuck in traffic, I'll have to leave my car and flee," she learned to say, "Sure I'm anxious. But I can always open a window, or play a tape to relax me."
5. She discovered the benefits of praising herself for every effort and attempt she made, anxiety and all.

It really doesn't matter how long the inner voice has plagued you with disaster fantasies. The important thing to remember is that you can change it, just as Jeanette did. This is something entirely within your power to alter; all you must do is become sensitive to what you tell yourself.

In cases like this, it's really important to quiet that inner voice and replace it with an accepting, soothing one. When I work with performers I try to help them tap their own wonderful storehouses of creative energy, which are theirs for the asking; this energy is merely being blocked by anxiety. Here it is essential for them to use artistic visualization to see in their minds how good auditioning can feel. I try to have them tune into positive anxiety without taking that extra step into intense stage fright.

Performers often insist: "But I've always thought in terms of disaster. Even as a child I'd get scared stiff over recitals, school plays, anything that had me performing!" "Yes," I reply, "but look at the profession you chose. You knew that you were talented and your fears never stopped you!" Performers need to give themselves a lot of credit for getting up before the audience or the cameras, butterflies, and all. I truly believe that the artistic temperament is one of the most powerful sources of energy around. All it really needs is to be unleashed, not hampered by undeserved anxiety.

Performers also need to focus in on all the lovely benefits of their talents, to get a realistic sense of the hard work, the years of experience, and the feelings of exhilaration when the applause and good reviews come in. All this results in positive, forward motion instead of paralyzing anxiety reinforced by thoughts of disaster.

The first step to keep in mind with the fear response is to minimize avoidance. When you avoid a situation or person, you fuel the fear; it's avoidance that increases fear's power.

Each time you approach a scary, anxiety-producing situation, use it to demonstrate that you're willing to take a risk to get over your fear. This courage should be rewarded by giving yourself the recognition and praise that your strength deserves. You're making the effort to move ahead, despite the fears.

Linda was quite outgoing in college and liked by the other students and faculty. At thirty-two she married George, a successful salesman, and after two years decided to have a child. Both Linda and George were ecstatic when their infant was born. She had decided to take a leave of absence from her job at a brokerage firm so that she could focus all her attention on raising her daughter. But she had some difficulty adjusting to her new role as housewife and mother, since she had enjoyed her job and the people she worked with.

One afternoon, while waiting in an unusually slow line at the bank, Linda experienced her first anxiety attack. Without any warning her heart began to pound rapidly and she felt dizzy. All she knew was that she had to get out of there—immediately! Unfortunately for Linda she did just that. Instead of tolerating the panicky feelings, she made a mad dash for her car.

An unexpected fear attack is a terrifying experience. You probably sympathize with Linda's desire to flee, yet this was the worst possible thing for her to do. After her first attack, she began to fear a repeat performance and thus began the avoidance-fear cycle. She began to dread and avoid places where an attack might recur, first banks, then restaurants, and then shopping malls.

When Linda first arrived in my office, she was depressed and feeling quite hopeless. Her husband drove her to the session, since she had recently developed a fear of driving.

Linda spoke of feeling worthless as a person and victimized by her fears. She couldn't imagine a normal life and was convinced that she would never be free from her anxieties. At that stage of treatment, her feelings were to be expected. Why should she have felt she could ever resume normal activities, or think of being free from panic, when panic was her constant companion?

The first steps to recovery were terribly frightening, but we took them slowly. On her first trip to the supermarket, Linda entered the store, yet found the panic too strong to remain there. It was important at this point for her to give herself credit for even venturing to the store.

She knew she was being victimized by the physical sensations that went along with the fears—the dizziness, trembling hands, pounding heart, and rubbery knees. But she eventually learned to stop adding to the anxiety by accepting these unpleasant symptoms and not being afraid of them. By accepting the sensations she lessened their intensity, and realized that avoidance was the number one friend of her fears, as it is for all anxieties and phobias.

I am not for one moment suggesting that you immediately try things that produce acute panic; such torture really isn't necessary. I want to show you, however, that taking these first, small steps is essential to your ultimate cure. As with anything, you'll need to practice in order to diminish the power of fear. If you practice getting out, even if it means exchanging a few words with a neighbor or store clerk, that's the path to success.

The issue I now want to explore with you is how to deal with your horrible, pessimistic thoughts so that you can begin to lead a normal life. The solution is not so much to try and fight them head on, but rather to develop techniques to switch the thoughts as soon as they invade any space of your mind. I suggest to patients that they envision a light switch they quickly turn off whenever they have unwanted thoughts. This stops the negative thoughts before they develop full force.

I want you to start introducing positive-outcome scenarios in order to purge the negative ones. This means both redoing your disaster vocabulary and, at the same time, using your creative powers to visualize successful endings. Positive energy used with imaginative skills can work wonders with a frazzled, anxious ego. Such successful scenarios tune you into your strengths and get you connected with the here and now.

Whenever Tommy, who owned a small retail business, had to confront customers who were late in paying their bills, he froze. The thought of facing them made him extremely tense.

He had inherited the business after his father's sudden death from heart failure. During high school and college, Tommy had worked for his father and saw how difficult it was for him, too, to confront anyone who owed him money. The father constantly swallowed his feelings and made excuses for late payers. "I've known him for years," he said of one. "He'll pay eventually." When Tommy took over the business, it was having a serious cash-flow problem. Yet he still hesitated to remind the debtors that they owed him money.

Tommy's hesitation came from a fear of being criticized. He went to great lengths to please people and avoided conflict at all costs. Unfortunately, he sacrificed himself in the process because of his need to be accepted. Finally his wife encouraged him to consult a therapist.

When I asked Tommy to act out the situation of

calling someone on an overdue bill, he became very anxious. Since he was quite assertive with his wife and friends, it was clear that his father's influence had made him turn to jelly in certain circumstances. We spoke at length about his feelings surrounding money, and what unpaid balances meant to him. The more aware he was of his behavior, the easier it was for him to recognize the learned response he inherited from his father. Tommy's inner voice was falsely telling him to be accepting of others' faults, and bear the burden of their troubles. "Forget about your needs for payment, sacrifice yourself for others. Then you'll be liked and accepted." The intent of his father's voice was to ensure that Tommy would follow in his footsteps.

It's important to begin to think of the old inner voice as an unwanted guest inhabiting your mind . . . a guest who has long overstayed his or her welcome. Instead of doubting yourself I want you to replace this tape with a kinder, gentler voice, one that is definitely on your side. To do this it's important to practice positive imagery. Instead of believing that catastrophe lurks around every corner, I want you to believe more in your own powers.

You're probably asking yourself: "How do I get rid of the old psychological tapes that have been with me for so long?" Let's begin right now. Close your eyes and focus on a scene . . .

For Tommy the scene was meeting one of the customers who owed him money. Tommy envisioned pointing out that the bill had been past due for four months and that he would appreciate a prompt payment. In his scene the customer apologized and immediately wrote out a check for the balance. He promised Tommy that he would keep his account current and that such behavior would not happen again.

Such visualization techniques are a potent force for liberating the power of the mind. A positive, can-do mental framework can have a profound effect,[1] and repeating over and over the positive attitude you want to acquire is the first step toward actually experiencing it. By using reassuring words and tones, you will feel more at ease in situations where you now feel uncomfortable. Talking assertively, calmly, confidently "stimulate[s] the production of a whole range of neurotransmitters, or brain hormones, which affect everything from alertness and concentration to depression."[2]

Moreover, controlling your facial muscles and posture as well as your voice to exude confidence will eventually result in a feeling of confidence. "Something as simple as a smile transmits nerve impulses to the limbic system, the emotional center of the brain. The result: positive feelings of happiness or relaxation."[3]

Another benefit of refocusing your anxious feelings is that you can become more in touch with your environment. You'll want to lessen your tendency to monitor every internal sensation and begin to enjoy the world around you. Feel the warmth of the sun, smell the air after a rainfall. Tune yourself into these pleasures instead of taking a magnifying glass to your fears.

If you have a tough day ahead of you, why not begin the morning with positive statements about yourself? Look at yourself in the mirror and genuinely learn to appreciate the reflection. Instead of observing negatives

—"My hair's graying; my wrinkles are appearing"— consider your smile or the twinkle in your eye.

Your external features are only the beginning. I want you to move toward getting a real sense of your inner pool of talents and abilities so that you can give yourself a new script to live and grow with.

CHAPTER FOURTEEN

NUTRITION
AND ANXIETY

YOU are what you eat. The foods, beverages, and medications you consume all have something in common: they affect you both physically and mentally. A recent article in *The New York Times* was one of many indicating causal links between the foods people eat and their mental well-being: "Tyrosine, which comes from protein such as that in meat or fish, led to subjects being in better moods and less anxious or tense."[1]

Believing that a cup of coffee "relaxes" you is a major mistake. People who suffer anxiety are greatly affected by caffeine, which in many cases can actually trigger more fear. Because caffeine "may sometimes bring on symptoms that mimic an anxiety attack,"[2] it is essential to evaluate your coffee habit and see whether it's perhaps the culprit behind your anxiety. *The Diagnostic and Statistical Manual of Mental Disorders III*, the official handbook for therapists, describes "Caffeinism" as a condition in which the sufferer is jittery and may tremble and feel anxious. If you are prone to anxiety, coffee can propel the fear cycle into action. You might feel shaky, or have an upset stomach or headache, and suddenly worry that it's just the beginning of a fear attack. In one study, just drinking black coffee in the morning led to lassitude, irritability, nervousness, hunger, fatigue, exhaustion, and headaches.[3] I don't want you to become obsessive if you like coffee, but be aware of the effects it might have on your behavior.

So what to do if you find that coffee causes more stress? If you are a heavy coffee drinker, consider cutting down gradually to avoid severe withdrawal symptoms. You may try to eliminate one or two cups a week at first, switching to other hot beverages, such as herbal tea, or decaffeinated coffee. Eventually you can become caffeine free, a wise choice if you are a fearful person who is "allergic" to caffeine.

Another area to investigate is your intake of sweets. If you have a highly sensitive nervous system, you may overreact to sugar. It could make you jumpy and has been known to cause sleep disturbances in children and some adults. If you're already an energetic person, stimulants like caffeine and sugar only increase your adrenalin. This is certainly not what you need.

"The typical diet of someone who comes to see us includes eight to ten cups of coffee a day, lots of sweets, and very few slow-release high-protein foods," says Alan Goldstein, Ph.D., Director of the Temple University Medical School Agoraphobia and Anxiety Center in Philadelphia. "They might have coffee and a doughnut for breakfast, more coffee at midmorning, a white-bread sandwich at lunch, and maybe a good supper. Then something sweet before they go to bed."[4] So it is understandable that your diet should be investigated for its anxiety-producing effects.

You may wonder why you feel jittery after taking certain prescription or over-the-counter medications. You may not understand why you can't sleep, or why your heart beats faster than usual. It's amazing how even common drugs and painkillers that are advertised on television have the effect of increasing your anxiety. For instance, weight-reducing pills may produce agitation because of their stimulants. Asthma medications have as possible side effects nervousness, rapid heartbeat, tremors, and nausea. Cold medications may lead to sleeplessness, rapid heartbeat, nervousness, and anxiety. Antihistamines can produce palpitations and excitation. Note the warnings of common side effects that appear on the labels of these drugs. You really don't need to add to your psychological symptoms.

In short, certain foods and drugs are to be scrutinized. Take a careful look at what you eat, to avoid the effects of a chemical reaction and to identify fears that do arise as a result of your having ingested certain foods or medications. This measure will allow you to take control and perhaps decrease some anxieties just by watching your diet. Caffeine, sugar, and certain medications are the foes of some people and should be avoided by you if necessary. It certainly isn't the end of the world to indulge your taste for sweets or coffee, but try to remember they can be powerful stimulants to a highly sensitive person.

So far I've been discussing some of the "dangers" of diet. But there are also things you can eat that encourage relaxation. It is well known that eating carbohydrates can make one feel relaxed, calm, and less depressed. Isn't it delightful to know that eating that plate of pasta with your favorite sauce can be good for you! Carbohydrates can definitely be seen as a friend to the anxious person. In addition to various foods, you can develop relaxing rituals around meals. Take time to enjoy your meal and, instead of gulping down your food, savor the taste and texture of the cuisine. Experiment with spices and try not to have the same sort of food again and again. Treat yourself to a pampered evening with candlelight and your favorite background music. Make it a relaxing event instead of a task to be performed because your body is hungry. This way you can create your own oasis, a respite from the day's tensions and worries.

I realize if you have children it's hardly possible to regularly dine this way, with an infant screaming and/or a teenager eager to leave the table for a television program or a phone call. But I'd like to emphasize the importance of making time, whether you live alone or have a family, to indulge yourself in this time-honored relaxation custom. With the culture moving toward fast food and more and more time spent eating on the run, you need to do, and deserve, more for yourself than this. Even if you can only treat yourself regally on occasion, I suggest strongly doing so. This way you can increase the feeling of well-being and reduce your stress and anxiety.

CHAPTER FIFTEEN

EXERCISING TO EXORCISE YOUR SYMPTOMS

EXERCISE. Everyone seems to be caught up in a fitness craze nowadays. Aerobic classes are everywhere and people spend their lunchtimes dancing. Jogging is in and rowing machine sales are up. One constantly hears how healthful it is to exercise, how valuable it is for burning up calories. For many people exercise is a part of an everyday regime to strengthen the cardiovascular system and reduce cholesterol.

In addition to the physical benefits, exercise is good

for your emotional well-being and can give you a feeling of euphoria. Physical activity produces natural tranquilizers in the brain. For the person suffering from fears, anxieties, or phobias, exercise can be an essential part of the program for relaxing.

There are plenty of additional bonuses tagged onto an exercise routine. Many fearful people dread the feeling of a pounding heart. As soon as their pulse starts racing, they're sure they're experiencing an anxiety attack. This thinking only serves to increase the adrenalin and bring on exactly the thing they fear most—panic. I want you to become acquainted with your body during exercise so that you don't add additional fear to your psychological state. As Dr. Claire Weeks put it, "To know that the thumping, racing, nervous heart is still under control, that it will not stop beating and will always revert to normal rhythm, helps the patient to regain confidence." Also, she states that exercise "abolishes" the sensation of missed heartbeats.[1]

There is also a strong correlation between hyperventilation and panic. True, some of the research is controversial, yet the fact remains: fearful people aren't the best deep breathers around! Evidence seems to point to poor breathing as one of the possible culprits behind panic. Accepting this fact, let's look at some of the findings. Current research suggests that in most instances symptoms precede the fear.[2] So exercise can help to make breathing easier and assist you to begin to take long, deep breaths that lead to relaxation. Breathing problems are notorious for anxious people since they tend to take short shallow breaths. With the help of exercise you'll learn to breath more deeply on a regular basis, which will bring more oxygen to the brain, thus reducing anxiety.

Think about your breathing for a moment and you'll see how closely related it is to your emotional state. We let out deep sighs of sadness and long sighs of relief. We take shallow, rapid breaths when we're scared, let out gasps of surprise, and shouts for joy.

If you suffer panicky fears, it may be that you often have trouble breathing and simply don't realize it. Hyperventilation can occur frequently for panic sufferers. Yet exercise and becoming more aware of your inhales and exhales can be enormously helpful in reducing panic. The long, deep breaths you take when you exercise can be brought on whenever you need extra oxygen!

A pounding heart can now become associated with the rigors and pleasures of exercise. You no longer have to assume that a racing pulse equals panic. I like to encourage patients to try a simple experiment: Do jumping jacks for five minutes and develop an awareness of your heartbeat. When you feel your heart pounding, look in the mirror and talk to yourself. You will see that you hardly look out of control and in fact appear quite fine. All of your fantasies of how you look to others when your heart is pounding are needless worries. Many fearful people find that once their heart starts to pound, the fear spiral starts. They can't utter a word because their throat closes up and their entire face quivers. So start demystifying these fears by watching yourself after exercise and you'll see that only when you add catastrophic language does the panic start. Your pounding heart and trembling limbs signal only that you've been exercising; you don't have to associate them with panic. Unfortunately for people who are out of shape, even walking up a flight of stairs can start the heart pounding, so they live in constant fear of that sensation, avoiding anything that will induce it.

It's important to remember a few key points here:

1. Just because your heart may pound or may feel like it skips a beat doesn't necessarily signal an anxiety attack.
2. Get acquainted with your body. Learn how it functions when you exercise, and apply this knowledge to everyday experiences.
3. Become more aware of your breathing. A simple exercise is to lie down and put a hardcover book on your abdomen. Then see if you can elevate the book by breathing deeply. If you don't see it lift much you may be suffering from hyperventilation. Remember too that with hyperventilation the symptom precedes the fear. So if you can learn more effective breathing you can greatly reduce your panic.
4. Moderate exercise can be good for you, both physically and psychologically.

So check with your physician and get his opinion on an exercise regime that is good for you. Then start a program that will help you to deemphasize your anxious symptoms as you move toward better health. Remind yourself that in addition to getting into good physical shape, you'll be developing good attitudes about yourself when you start exercising and taking care of your body. During workouts that get your heart going at an increased rate, you'll learn that the heart is merely functioning normally. You can then become more familiar with how it works, and not see it as an anxiety trigger.

Exercise can also increase your energy, which may be depleted from battling the fear response, and it will help you feel that you are doing something positive for yourself. Remember that exercise and nutrition can be useful tools to diminish the fear response.

PART THREE

STAYING
FEAR-LESS

IN these last chapters we're going to explore how to maintain and enjoy your inner strength. I've spoken about what your fears are and how they evolved. After that, we looked at diet, nutrition, changing the inner voice, and accepting yourself. All of these discussions were designed to get you on the right path. Now it's time to see what you'll need to stay in top-flight psychological health!

You're ready to start seeing the value of praise and how affirming yourself can be essential for keeping you in touch with your strengths. Yet acceptance also means allowing for the possibility of recurrence. Your symptoms may never reappear, but if they do it won't throw you—you'll know the episode will be merely temporary and will give you the opportunity to exhibit your newly acquired power.

I'm also going to give you tips on raising children who aren't afraid to assert themselves and can take risks by performing in school plays, speaking up in class, and dealing with other children who might be attacking and hostile.

Finally, we arrive at the tremendous importance of learning to love the nonfearful you. An essential part of the program is to emphasize your unique traits and characteristics.

You've worked hard to overcome your fears. That's why I'm going to stress the absolute importance of loving the courage and determination that are now a permanent part of you.

CHAPTER SIXTEEN

REWARDING
AND PRAISING
YOURSELF

> Courage is doing what you're afraid to do.
> There can be no courage unless you're afraid.
> —Edward Rickenbacker

IT'S really quite important to treat yourself grandly when you work through your fear, anxiety, or phobia. For every time you took a risk and boarded the plane despite your fear, or stepped into that forbidden supermarket where panic seized you a few short months ago, you need to reward yourself. If you're saying to yourself, "So I went to the supermarket just like millions of people do every day. Big deal! I should have been able to have walked in there without panic to begin with," you're doing yourself an injustice.

It *is* a big deal if you've been frightened of shopping, driving, or taking an elevator and did it anyway. You very much need to acknowledge it. Without giving yourself credit you're depriving yourself not only of the immediate reward for trying something that's scary, but also hindering your future progress. It's essential for your continued growth to recognize that although something previously caused you fear and trepidation, you took a risk and did it anyway!

Dan, an electronics engineer in his mid-thirties who worked for a large Midwestern firm, had an awful fear of speaking in public. In college he had to take a course in public speaking and dreaded it beyond belief. The six speeches he was required to make in class sent him into a state of panic. He didn't have any trouble with interviews and small group discussions, yet the thought of presenting before an "audience" made his heart race and his hands sweat. This fear carried over into his present job. Every time his boss looked for volunteers to speak on social issues before community groups, Dan always had an excuse for why he couldn't participate. Avoidance and fear ruled his life. Yet one day Dan had no choice. His boss told him that in three weeks he was to represent the company at the regional sales meeting and present the plans for an upcoming merger. Dan was terrified. He spent sleepless nights obsessing over how foolish he'd look in front of everyone. It made his life miserable and caused friction with his wife, Martha. Her efforts to reassure Dan were fruitless; both felt at their wit's end. Dan decided he would keep his presentation short and to the point, so he could escape more quickly to the safety of his seat, jangled nerves and all.

Finally, after confiding in a close friend, he was referred to me. His friend had had a similar problem and was helped immensely by treatment. Dan felt a glimmer of hope. After lots of work, he felt somewhat armed with therapeutic help. He went to the meeting, keeping in mind my advice to him: "Don't examine all your fear sensations. Focus on speaking to one person in the audience, and even as you look around, remember this person is on your side." I had also said, "I'll be thinking of you and look forward to hearing about how you did!" Dan felt that I understood, and that his symptoms were not crazy. He sailed through the meeting, sweaty palms and all, and found himself fatigued yet elated. He also recalled my advice to reward himself if he felt successful and not to blame himself if things did not go well this time—there's always tomorrow. Since Dan felt it was a performance well done, he took a swim in the hotel pool where the meeting took place, and booked himself into an elegant restaurant for dinner. In other words, he rewarded himself for pushing through the fear situation, which he had every right to do.

Too often we diminish our accomplishments and take them for granted. Whoever thinks, "So what if I haven't driven across a bridge for three years. It's about time I grow up," does herself a disservice by making her attempts less important than they are. It's akin to someone who can't accept a compliment yet will be the first to hear criticism. You need to feel good about every attempt. If you believe that the only way you can feel you accomplished something is if you handle every situation anxiety free, then your struggle becomes a long, lonely uphill battle that has too few treats along the way.

Rewarding yourself for risk taking can be very personal, and you need to identify what it is that would make you feel better. For Dan, it was a swim, followed by a superb dinner, where he could feel catered to. For you it may be a new suit, or even a bouquet of fresh flowers. Rewards such as these bring home the reality of what you've done, despite your anxiety, and remind you of how much you deserve.

Agatha hated elevators, but loved to collect antiques, so when she took her first elevator ride to the next floor, I encouraged her to buy the antique inkwell she had been eager to buy for several weeks. At first she tried to downplay her accomplishment. This tendency is very typical of the fearful person. Often, they are their own worst critics, ready to seize on every flaw in themselves and unwilling to indulge in rewarding their efforts.

If you're like Agatha, you should try to work through this resistance; it's necessary to praise yourself and start conditioning yourself to enjoyment and pleasure. After all, you've earned it! Moreover, when you think negatively and deprive yourself of the credit you deserve, you deprive yourself of the positive reinforcement that is needed to continue your progress. So try saying, "I like my courage and I'm proud of me for trying."

Praise is an important way to enhance and solidify your victory over the fear response. It can come from friends, relatives, colleagues, and, most important, yourself. How fantastic to know someone respects you for trying! How nice to hear someone say, "I think it's really super that you signed your name on the check in the bank. I know how frightening it is for you!" For all who battle anxiety, praise helps cure the dreaded fear response, since it acknowledges that others are rooting for you. Indeed we all want to hear that we're doing okay, and not have our vulnerabilities pointed out to us, but this is particularly true of fearful people. You already do a good enough job in the criticism department yourself, without having more heaped on you.

I'd like you to begin turning to people who are supportive of you and asking them to tell you how much they appreciate your achievements. Asking for something is a way of asserting and accepting yourself. Tuning into your needs and finding ways to meet them will have wonderful consequences for you.

CHAPTER SEVENTEEN

DEALING
WITH HOSTILES

All cruelty springs from weakness.
—Seneca

ONE of the most frustrating, infuriating, and anxiety-provoking experiences is to be face to face with angry, belligerent people. And, alas, there's more than a small share of them around. When you're sensitive and intuitive, you tend to react more to people like this than do people who are better insulated, and perhaps more hostile themselves. You sense their arrogance and you wilt rather than deal with your own aggressive feeings toward these clowns.

Fearful people often dread being around bitter, offensive individuals. They find criticism devastating, and have trouble realizing that attacks are not their problem but the problem of the attacker. If you're fearful, you know how anxious you are to escape from anyone who might be emotionally bruising. The feelings such people generate seem beyond what your body and psyche can tolerate. Yet the reality is that escape is not always possible.

Aurora, a high school teacher, was a sensitive, gifted woman who suffered from the fear response. She enjoyed beautiful clothes and spent her summers traveling to various parts of the world. Yet her colleagues seethed with envy. "Another new dress, Aurora? Your cleaning bills must kill you."

As the end of the school year approached, she heard other attacks. "Where are you going this summer, Aurora? You must spend your entire salary on your trips."

Aurora would recoil with anxiety. She dreaded these comments and fretted continually to me about, "What if Ken comments about my trip this summer? Or if Dorothy makes a remark about my new outfit? What would I say?"

I pointed out to Aurora that people are envious and she doesn't need to be allergic to their criticisms. She has enormous strength and ability to deal with people's hostile comments and their envy.

Aurora needed to practice not doubting herself when envious, snide remarks were made. Instead of asking herself, "Do I spend too much on clothes and traveling?" she needed to see these attacks as the problems of others, not hers. After all, she saved her money carefully and was entitled to spend it any way she liked. Aurora enjoyed esthetic pleasures that included a sense of fashion, and loved expanding her experiences by traveling.

She learned to see the value of making affirmative statements about her choices. Her doubts about herself and her fears of being attacked lessened when she took care of other people's hostility. "Oh, do you like silk? I love it." "Yes, I had a lovely time and I'm looking forward to returning next summer. What are you doing?"

Fearful people need not be victimized by denouncers. Hostile people show their true colors in a thousand different ways. But you don't have to be allergic to their attacks.

If you have an obnoxious co-worker who complains about everything, you won't be able to make your excuses, since you work in the same office five days a week. Even if you're tired of hearing the same old tirade, you may feel you have no choice but to be passive and listen to the gripes. The reality is that sometimes you do have a choice, although you're probably thinking, "Sure I do—I can get fired or transferred."

I'm not suggesting that you do anything to jeopardize your job or yourself. There is, however, another alternative, and this lies within you and your ability to tune into your feelings: you need to *express* those feelings to yourself instead of *repressing* them. By repression I mean denying your reaction to the situation, which only causes you to feel anxious every time you think of it. Instead you can begin to accept that you can't stand your co-worker, and the next time your heart pounds in his or her presence, you can tune into the fact that you're angry, annoyed, or irritated. You can think how much you would like to tell this bore off, yet acknowledge that you're working in the same place and temporarily stuck, unless of course, you decide to look for another job. Getting another position may be the answer, but an alternative goal is to tolerate your feelings, and learn to deal with people you dislike.

In short, the solution to the problem is tuning into your feelings and allowing yourself to fantasize. Let's face it: hostile, arrogant people are anywhere and everywhere. In fact, they may also be at your next job.

Perhaps your everyday dealing with telephone operators, taxi drivers, and store clerks, may seem like an overwhelming challenge to your emotional stability. Again, angry people show up in all places, from the vice-president in charge of operations to the next-door neighbor. The important thing to realize is that your allergic reaction to them need not be so strong and that you can develop strategies that will help you keep your sanity and not throw you off balance.

Take Laurie, for example. She dreaded going to parties with more than a few people at them, especially if they were people she didn't know. Whenever someone approached her to chat it felt like torture, yet she also hated standing around in silence. She had a terrible fear of blushing and perspiring and was petrified that everyone would see it. "What if someone shakes my hand and I'm drenched with sweat?" she fretted, "I'll give myself away in an instant!"

Christmas signaled the best and the worst for her. Parties were everywhere and the invitations always poured in. Her initial impulse was to decline them yet she didn't want others to know that she was avoiding. Her solution was to stay for half an hour and then make her excuses. She kept her coat close at hand so that she could easily slip away, hoping no one would see, but always for the person who suffers such anxiety, there's one in the crowd who does take notice and points out the behavior in a condescending manner.

Sure enough, at the office party a tall, recently divorced salesman, Doug, aggressively headed toward Laurie and in a loud voice said, "Laurie, is anything wrong? Every time I see you, you're either hugging the wall or grabbing your coat. Why don't you stay awhile instead of bolting for the door?"

Laurie felt exposed and completely humiliated. She was sure the entire party had overheard his remarks and feared that she would be the object of ridicule. Her mind went blank, but she managed to utter a few words, although she felt her throat closing up: "I have to visit my sister tonight." Taking advantage of a moment when he was distracted, she slipped out, hurrying down the stairs in fear that he or someone else would call after her. On her way home all she could picture was how he would make fun of her and talk about her to her co-workers. She imagined him saying, "What's wrong with Laurie? She can never stay and have a good time. I never get to say more than a few words to her and she's off making a beeline for the door."

The tears streamed down Laurie's face as she resigned herself to avoiding parties for the rest of her life rather than risk being humiliated again. Ever since she was a child she got anxious at parties. She felt she'd looked foolish reaching for a glass with trembling hands or else drop the dip on the floor. She knew she would betray her nervousness; being asked to dance was enough to send her into despair. She feared she would perspire and that all the deodorant in the world wouldn't save her. Yet as much as she feared get-togethers she yearned to be included.

What Laurie failed to recognize, and give herself credit for, was that she did not avoid the parties, despite her fears. Instead of making excuses, she went, even if she stayed only a short while. In addition to deserving a pat on the back, she had to learn more effective techniques for dealing with hostile people. Types like Doug will always be around, if not at one party, then at the next. It was important for Laurie to have responses ready for situations when her anxiety was pointed out, and of course, ultimately, to stay longer and longer without making excuses.

As we worked on Laurie's fears, it became clear that she associated parties with the fear that someone would verbally attack her for her symptoms. She soon got to the point where it no longer mattered if a hostile person made a jab at her. She realized plenty of people respected and cared for her, connected with the positive energy of her friends, and developed techniques for dealing with the Dougs of the world.

One of the things that a fearful person dreads the most is having a head-to-head confrontation with a Nasty. Anxiety causes them to deny and explain away some of the angry behavior of people, or else they make tremendous efforts to avoid such people, which may also result in the avoidance of activities, places, and people they enjoy.

Nancy had a tremendous fear that people would notice she perspired heavily when she got anxious. She dreaded someone would call attention to this and make fun of her, saying, "My God, it's twenty degrees outside.

How come you're sweating so much?" As soon as she felt even a tinge of anxiety, her confidence waned and she felt exposed by her perspiration.

Nancy's anxiety reached an all-time high when she faced an upcoming job interview. The morning of the interview, she woke up with butterflies in her stomach and a slight headache. Her sleep had been interrupted by nightmares of fainting and crumbling in front of people, or, in her words, "looking like a nervous wreck." She knew she was worried about how she would come across in the interview and imagined herself "sweating like a pig."

The interviewer was a woman about ten years older than Nancy and quite competitive and cold. She seemed to enjoy making Nancy feel uncomfortable as she asked intrusive questions. Nancy's worst fears were realized. She began to perspire heavily, not just under her arms but on her face and hands as well. She debated between using a handkerchief and possibly drawing attention to herself, or having sweat beads form on her face. Her anxiety skyrocketed as she thought, "Oh no! I know she sees me sweating. I know how stupid I look!" Sure enough, the hostile woman turned from her notetaking and inquired, "Is anything wrong? You seem to be so tense." She said this in such a critical manner that Nancy wanted to run away as fast as she could. She felt exposed and foolish. After the interview, she berated herself for going. "Why didn't I just stay at home today and not put myself through this?" She even considered staying at her present job, although there was no advancement in sight. She felt hopeless and depressed rather than angry at being treated so rudely at the interview by such an insensitive boor.

Nancy had to learn that anyone who would call attention to her anxiety doesn't score high on the humanity list, and doesn't deserve the power that Nancy gave her. All Nancy had to do was get the job, since she wouldn't be working with this woman anyway.

This is an important point to remember when you're dealing with angry, attacking people. Get in touch with who you are and what your goals are, not what a hostile person feels toward you. Too often fearful people feel so humiliated about their anxiety that the thought of someone calling attention to it makes it much worse. It's possible to reach a point of simply not caring about what someone says about your symptoms. Nancy cared too much about other people's opinions of her, and used them as a basis for her own feelings about herself. She hated herself when she looked vulnerable or scared, particularly if someone said something about her perspiration problem. By learning that plenty of people are ready to draw attention to someone else's vulnerability, you can recognize that such behavior says a lot about them, and very little about you. You'll see that it's their problems that make them envious and offensive.

I suggested to Nancy that she practice going to interviews, even if she wasn't interested in the job. We prepared her for an eventual interview for a desirable position, including responses to hostility, if they were required. Sure enough, she ran into a man who sat behind his huge oak desk, peering over his half-glasses as if he were examining her every move. When he commented on her anxiety—"Is anything the matter? I see you're hands are shaking and you're perspiring a lot for someone in an air-conditioned room."—Nancy was primed and ready to do battle! She turned his hostile remark around and asked him, "Aren't you accustomed to seeing people get anxious in an interview?" He was flustered and began to shuffle his papers. His aim had been to humiliate her, and he hadn't expected an assertive response. She left the interview feeling exhilarated and couldn't have cared less whether she landed the job. She knew in her heart that she was the winner.

The cases of Laurie and Nancy illustrate certain points to remember when you encounter hostile people:

1. Don't make excuses for their behavior and turn your justified anger against yourself. They have no right to attack you and you have nothing to be ashamed about!
2. Turn their intrusive questions back on them, just as Nancy did. Practice what you might say if someone comments on your anxiety in an offensive way. Have a response ready so that you fluster him or her a bit.
3. Allow yourself to be angry! This is not easy when one is fearful, since sensitive people experience anger as a negative emotion; it makes them feel uncomfortable.

Donald had a fierce phobia about blushing. From the time he was a child, people pointed at his beet-red face and made fun of it. "Look at him blush!" was a cry as familiar to him as his name. As a result he was not very outgoing, had difficulty asking someone for a date, and felt awkward at work. He occupied a middle-management position in a small accounting firm in the Southwest, and knew that if he were more assertive he could start an independent business and be his own boss. Unfortunately, because of his anxiety about blushing and fear that clients would comment on it, he stayed in a safe job with a steady salary.

Donald never learned how to deal with hostile people who really should have been confronted. When, as a child, he had confided in his mother about the taunts of other children she made excuses for them, such as, "Oh, I'm sure Paul didn't mean that. You know how much he likes playing ball with you." So Donald learned passivity and turned the other cheek rather than tune into his feelings.

This behavior carried over into adulthood. Donald excused other people who called attention to his blushing, but continued to feel devastated. He wasn't in touch with the recognition that anyone who would even mention his blushing was an angry, attacking person, and hardly someone he should choose to spend an evening with! By denying his own aggressive feelings, his anxiety soared.

Although some people may comment about blushing or shyness or perspiration out of concern, rather than malice or insensitivity, it's important to trust your feelings and judge how a remark is intended. Think about it for a moment: would you make comments to someone whose face turned red? For Donald blushing was the source of intense embarrassment. He was fortunate to acknowledge his need for help to cope with his feelings.

Once again, as with Nancy, Donald had to practice appropriate responses when confronted with hostile behavior. He learned to tune into his anger and have some good snappy things to say to hostile remarks. Donald discussed this problem with his group and discovered several creative ways to deal with such crude remarks. Now whenever someone commented on his reddened face and neck, he retorted, "I'm just exercising my blood vessels." Eventually he stopped caring so much about the blushing and put his anxiety into perspective, which resulted in a reduction in his blushing.

The important things in life are a strong value system, good relationships, and such qualities as sensitivity, compassion, and responsibility. Your trembling hands, rubbery legs, stuttering, blushing, or perspiring have nothing to do with the real you. You need to develop a good perspective of who you are and what your inner life is all about. This way you can begin to care less about other people's reactions to your fears.

Whenever Eleanor called a store to get clarification about an order she placed or to inquire about her bill, she was overcome with anxiety. As happens to all of us, she would often get a busy signal, or be put on hold. Then a harsh voice would answer, sounding as if Eleanor had no right to call. These everyday annoyances are frustrating and require you to develop coping skills, so that the frustrations don't trip you up and take you into the anxiety realm.

Eleanor needed to acknowledge her right to call and ask questions, and that these minor annoyances were not worth feeling anxious about. As she developed assertive techniques, she felt less fearful and accomplished more.

Remind yourself of these important facts, especially when you evaluate yourself by your symptoms. If people chide you for your fear of dogs, or act superior because they don't suffer from the fear response, it's their problem, not yours! If they can mistreat a sensitive person, you can wager that their ability to have good relationships with other people is rather slim. How they treat you is indicative of how they relate to the world. You need to practice ways of behaving and responding that protect yourself from hostile comments. Disregarding criticism from people who don't deserve the time of day is a useful lesson to learn, especially for sensitive people, who put too much stock in the comments of others.

Practice certain responses if you know you're vulnerable to those who call attention to your fears:

1. Rehearse lines that you can toss out if someone calls attention to your anxiety. Kimberly felt humiliated every time someone remarked about her stuttering. She learned to have a response ready in case something was said about it: "I always stutter when I feel intense, and I like it! So what?"

   If you fear hostile people will draw attention to your trembling hands, you'll need a response that matches their hostility. Erika found it helpful to say, "I just found out that I've got a bad virus." After that she felt more in control since she saw the attackers become a little upset wondering whether they'd catch it.

   Barbara always had a difficult time with cab drivers in New York. She found some of them rude and was annoyed by their aggressive driving. Her heart would pound and she felt she couldn't breathe. Her solution to cabbies who asked her why she kept the window open and seemed so nervous was to say, "I'm tired after jet lag. Those European trips are so exhausting!"

2. See the individuals who make the comment as being angry, inappropriate persons who never learned manners. Instead of giving them power over you, recognize that their comments are rude and intrusive. Try to describe them in a phrase to yourself—boor, nerd, jerk—anything that helps you to put the situation into perspective and not feel so affected.

3. Understand their motives. They're attempting to make you feel self-conscious and humiliated. Their own feelings of bitterness, unhappiness, and inferiority lead them to act like bullies who try to make others feel uncomfortable. Avoid asking yourself, "What's wrong with me?" Instead ask, what's wrong with *them*?

4. Most important, tune into the way you feel in these situations and try not to turn it on yourself. When a person is obnoxious, you have every right to be furious. Let me repeat this point because fearful people are notorious for ignoring their feelings and pretending that they aren't angry, what psychologists call "denial." Denial is especially harmful when you're confronted with an angry bully; you have every right to all your feelings.

5. It's helpful to fantasize about what you'd like to really say (or do) to a hostile person! Fantasizing is not the same as acting on impulse, and no one has ever been arrested for thinking

about strangling someone. Imagining stringing up a bully from the nearest lamppost can go a long way in helping you to get in touch with your feelings toward that person. Learn to admit to your aggressive feelings and even start to enjoy them!

CHAPTER EIGHTEEN

RECURRENCE: JUST ANOTHER CHALLENGE

SYMPTOM recurrence is something that happens. It's awful when it does, yet it's also a necessary part of the ultimate cure. Just when you think, "Thank God I'm past it," the symptoms show up again. You wake up with anticipatory anxiety in the morning when you thought you'd conquered your leaving-the-house fear. The thought of a sales presentation with its old familiar anxiety is enough to make you feel like screaming. You honestly believed you were past the old bugaboo, and suddenly it's back. You thought you had conquered the fear response and now it's returned with a vengeance!

It feels worse than ever for you, since you were doing things, going places, and meeting people without that excess fearful baggage. When the fear returns you feel hopeless and to a certain extent more discouraged than ever. This is because *you know how life is without fearful thoughts and feelings.*

I want to remind you that recurrence doesn't mean you're right back where you started. It simply means that for a variety of reasons you're feeling vulnerable again. You have to instruct yourself in the same techniques that helped you through the first time.

"Setbacks," as Dr. Claire Weeks says, "could occur as a result of some strain, some tension may have slightly sensitized you once more."[1] It is enormously important to see recurrence as a challenge and not a defeat. It is a sign that you are conquering the enemy. Once more you have the opportunity of combatting the anxiety that tries to limit your potential, frighten you out of your wits, or cause you undo heartache. When you face the enemy square on and say to yourself, "It's back but not for long!" you diminish the power of its threat. Each time you pass another obstacle you strengthen yourself. The fear response has power over you only as long as you dread it. When you allow it to "wash over you," as Dr. Weeks says, and don't resist the impact, it lessens.

1. Recurrence is common and not to be feared.
2. The return of fear symptoms is a challenge. Meeting it will eventually allow you to over-

come your fears and stop looking over your shoulder wondering when and if the symptoms will return.

3. The fear response is worked through only when you don't live in fear of the physical feelings that are produced. Instead, *accept* the anxiety and flow with the symptoms.

4. The ultimate cure is learning to handle the anxiety without the additional fear of being scared about it returning.

5. Do not obsessively judge yourself by your symptoms, or by perfectionistic standards designed only to make you feel "different" from everyone else and thus "crazy."

Recurrence can very likely occur, particularly if you're more stressed than usual, or even recovering from an illness as insignificant as a mild cold. Your psyche becomes more sensitive at particular times for a variety of reasons, but the important thing to remember is to accept setbacks without being angry at yourself. You don't expect a life free from the common cold; you don't say to to yourself, "Great! This is the last flu I'll ever get!" Psychological symptoms also occur again. Just remember that recurrence does happen and that it is merely a temporary condition. Thinking this way helps to reduce the hopelessness and frustration of having the same old symptoms around, and helps you to get on the right path again.

I know that just as you begin to experience a life free from fear and anxiety, you will desperately want to feel this way all the time. Who wouldn't? Yet the ultimate cure lies in accepting these fearful feelings and not holding a barometer up to the sensations so that you start monitoring again.

I understand that even as you read my words, you may be thinking, "She can't possibly know how hopeless and vulnerable I feel. I really believed this time I was through with feeling fearful." I want you to know that I do very much recognize the pain you feel when you have such a relapse. It's debilitating and most certainly discouraging. But I want also to emphasize two points:

1. It's temporary, not forever.
2. It's a sign of how much progress you have made. Now you really know what potential awaits you out there.

I want you to remember these points because you need to be anchored in hope and not despair. Just as your strength of character got you past the fear response before, this same quality will be called upon to assist you again. Recurrence can't harm you; it serves to help you in the long run. As long as you see it as a mere temporary setback and nothing to get alarmed about, you'll win over it.

Jill was a stockbroker on Wall Street who had multiple phobic symptoms ranging from anxiety at speaking at presentations to a tremendous fear of flying. The symptoms plagued her for years, and her life revolved around her fears. She refused a job that required any public speaking, and traveled only to areas that she could reach by bus or train. Then taking elevators became torture and her anxieties completely ruled her life. She finally sought treatment and made significant progress in group therapy.

Although presentations were still anxious for her, she was able to fly to California from New York, and seriously considered a job that required presentations three times a year. For about six months she was revelling in her accomplishments. Then one Friday afternoon, after a particularly stressful week, she was about to board a plane with her husband for a relaxing weekend in Montreal, when suddenly that old queasy feeling hit. She thought that it was almost impossible to board the plane, but she did it anyway. Every moment was sheer torture, but she managed to get to Montreal, fantasies and all. Shaking with fear, her mind raced with alternative plans for getting back to New York. However, her husband wouldn't hear of it and insisted that she fly back with him as scheduled. At first she was furious with him, but as the weekend went on she felt a little better about it. When Sunday night came and the flight was announced, she decided that she would probably be a nervous wreck, but try it anyway. Sure enough her stomach churned and she trembled from head to foot, but with her husband's encouragement she managed to get on the plane. The old anxiety was there, all right, but Jill remembered what we had spoken about and relied on the technique of letting the panic pass. Within a few minutes she was much better, although not totally calm. She was able to get through it by allowing herself to be fearful again without adding a lot of fantasies.

As Claire Weeks said, "Because this confidence has been borne the hard way, from your own experience, you will never quite lose it. You may falter, but you will never be completely overwhelmed again."[2] Jill's next step was to deal with her despair about her setback. Just as she thought she had conquered the phobic response, it hit her again. She actually felt worse, since she'd been free of the anxiety for awhile.

Once again, the important things to remember if this happens to you are the following:

1. Setbacks are only temporary.
2. The same courage that helped you to overcome your fears will assist you again.
3. Not only are recurrences common, they are also to be somewhat expected if you are stressed.
4. Try to see them as an opportunity to practice the skills which helped you to overcome your fears in the first place.

CHAPTER NINETEEN

RAISING ANXIETY-FREE CHILDREN

NEARLY all parents with fears are understandably concerned about passing them on to their children. The thought terrifies them; they understand too well the pain that anxiety causes and have no wish to make it an inheritance. I am frequently asked the question, "How can I prevent my son or daughter from developing these crazy fears? It's bad enough I have them without thinking my child will develop them too."

These concerned parents fret about whether anxiety

might be genetic. If so, they think, the poor child is doomed. They attack themselves for their "foolish" fears and worry that the child might be aware of them: "Other parents go to PTA meetings and drive their child to school. I can't imagine doing that, and I'm sure my daughter knows."

Current research on phobic disorders indicates that there may well be a genetic predisposition to the development of a phobia. Yet there is a strong learned response as well. You can't change your genes but you can model some styles of behavior to prevent fears from developing in your children. Even while you're still feeling anxious, you can alter what you say about your fears to your youngster.

Georgia was in the throes of a severe restaurant phobia before she consulted me. It had begun just after her divorce a few months earlier. She couldn't even go near a cafeteria or delicatessen to order a sandwich without having tremendous anxiety. Going out for a slice of pizza seemed impossible, so the food was delivered. In the previous few months, even buying an ice cream cone at a take-out counter became too much for her. By the time she came to see me she was beside herself with guilt. Her daughter Sarah was an avid lover of both pizza and ice cream, as befitted a five-year-old, but was too young to order for herself. Terrified of standing at the local ice cream counter, Georgia made excuses to her daughter: "Ice cream isn't good for your teeth," and, "It's too far to drive." But none of this reduced Sarah's insistence: "Karen's mommy gives her ice cream cones. Why can't I have them too?" In this case Karen actually helped her mother. How do you explain to a five-year-old about a restaurant phobia?

Georgia felt she had to seek treatment because her feelings for her daughter were stronger than the phobia.

It's not uncommon for a mother with a driving fear to get in the car if the school calls and says her child is sick. So the ability and resourcefulness is there; it's a matter of recognizing and using it.

But what happens when a child hears you and your spouse arguing about your avoidance? She wants to go on vacation to the Caribbean and you have a fear of flying. You might admit to another adult that you're not crazy about flying, but what do you say to your child?

Linda and Jack were asked by their eleven-year-old son, Cary, why they never took plane trips like his friends' families did. This came after a heated argument Linda and Jack had had over a trip to Europe that Linda wanted desperately to take. Yet Jack had a flying fear. At the dinner table Cary asked why they couldn't go to Europe, and Jack became noticeably anxious. He made feeble excuses: "I can't take off from work right now. Besides, it's an expensive time to go." (In fact, Jack owned his own business and was quite successful.) Both he and Linda were concerned about the question and over the next few days talked a lot about what they could say.

Jack finally decided to share with his son what was going on. He said that he wanted to talk about why they didn't travel the way their friends did: "Sometimes we feel scared of things even when there's no reason to. Well, I feel a little frightened of flying, but I know I'll get over it soon. I hate not doing these things, but I know it won't be long before we all travel a lot more. I just have to be anxious and do it anyway, I guess."

Cary's response indicated a lot of sensitivity. "Oh I know what you mean. Remember when we lived in the other house on Concord Street, and I hated having the lights out? Now it can be pitch black and it's okay." Jack was so impressed by his son's awareness that he was motivated to join a phobic group to overcome his fears about flying. Within a few months he was able to board a plane from New York to Washington, D.C., and within another few months scheduled a trip to London.

The perceptive eye of the child is hard to deceive. Such excuses as "The Ferris wheel can be dangerous," or, "We don't need to go to the top of the Empire State Building—we've seen plenty of pictures," may not be believed. Meanwhile your child easily gets the message: You're staying away from anything high up. Yet you don't need to continue to make excuses. Instead you could explain your phobia, as Jack did to Cary, and realize it's not the end of the world and that your child may even empathize with your fears. After all, children have fears too.

If you are a sincere and loving parent, you've already created a good foundation for your children to love you, vulnerabilities and all. These things can be explained to your child in a caring, loving fashion. Be aware of his or her feelings. It's not hard to explain in language a child can understand, and in a manner that he or she can relate to, what's going on. You don't need to belabor the point, but a little information can go a long way.

Sometimes knowing how much you want only the very best for your child can help in overcoming your fears. As I mentioned before, many a parent with a driving phobia will suddenly drive to school because a child is sick. Just knowing your child needs a model to look up to can tune you into your own strength.

In terms of helping your children to avoid inheriting your fears and phobias, it's essential that you don't try to protect them by being overly cautious. You may be fearful of elevators, but by continually avoiding them you risk having your child identify with your fear. You may dread social gatherings and meeting new people, but you can be quite encouraging when your child is asked to a classmate's birthday party. Even if you have a travel phobia I would recommend encouraging your son or daughter to take class trips, or overnight outings with Scouts or friends. Encourage them to socialize and go out for sports. Ask yourself what you needed when you were a child that would have lessened your anxiety. Just as I've spoken about how you can become a good parent to yourself, so you can become a soothing, encouraging parent to your child. Children need good role models, especially these days when heroes are somewhat scarce!

You can encourage your children to be assertive and not fearful of their feelings. Praise them when they try out for the school play, or help them with their oral presentations. That way they won't become afraid of making speeches, although you may dread them like the plague.

The following guidelines can be used as preventive measures:

1. Try not to talk much about your fears around your child, since somes fears, as you know, can be psychologically contagious.

2. If your fears are obvious, do the following: (a) admit your fears; (b) acknowledge that they don't make sense; (c) do it in a casual way to avoid causing your child undue anxiety; and (d) reassure your child that you have confidence that you can overcome them.

3. Continually encourage your child to take healthy risks, even when he or she feels trepidation. Children feel good when they've accomplished something in spite of their fear!

CHAPTER TWENTY

LOVING THE NONFEARFUL YOU

> In quiet we had learned to dwell,
> My very chains and I grew friends.
> So much a long communion tends
> To make us what we are:—even I
> regained my freedom with a sigh.
> —Byron, "The Prisoner of
> Chillon"

YOU have every right to be proud. It's been six months now since you've had intense fears, and maybe two months since your last panic. You remember dreading speaking in front of colleagues and now you do it with only a twinge of normal anxiety. You recall when driving across that ominous bridge seemed unbearable; now it's easy. Congratulations are definitely in order. You've worked hard and demonstrated tremendous courage. It's time to celebrate, to give yourself a good pat on the back and, in fact, fully process your gain.

You need to appreciate the struggle it took to overcome your fears, and to really get an integrated sense of who you are. Anyone who has worked through a fear or anxiety knows how incredibly difficult it was for you to overcome obsessing about your fears. At times it took every ounce of energy and a lot of discipline and determination to change that inner voice. You forced yourself to think differently about the world—to become an assertive person. And finally, you erased those old tapes from the past. Those that say "I can't," "I'll look foolish," or "I'll go crazy" are only occasionally part of your present.

This may sound hard to believe, but you're a hero who displayed a lot of bravery. The determined work that you've done needs to be respected. You have every right to feel proud when you take a plane, or go to a restaurant, or attend a singles' get-together. These are the rewards that await you when you put down the additional baggage of fears.

Emily, a thirty-year-old copywriter for a Madison Avenue advertising firm, developed a fear of oral presentations. It started when she was about to present her ideas in front of thirty people. Panic seized her. She pretended to have a sudden attack of the flu and managed to get out of the meeting, rubbery legs and all. She rushed to her general physician, who prescribed tranquilizers. Since Emily hated taking them, she resolved to do away with both the tranquilizers and the fear response. We worked hard together, and Emily was symptom-free within a year. Within four months she was given a substantial raise in salary and a promotion to go with it. She felt like a new person as she approached presentations with a newfound confidence. All those positive changes enhanced a revised view of herself as a competent, professional woman. But she didn't want to celebrate her accomplishments. When people noticed the changes, she changed the subject or dismissed their compliments lightly. Emily needed to accept the work and determination that enabled her to appreciate herself. Only then could she trust herself and enjoy her achievements.

There are all sorts of opportunities that await you when the quivering fear ceases. A new world opens up for you with new possibilities because you're not letting fear block your path.

It's really important to get to know yourself again. Imagine the exhilaration of walking into a bank and signing your name on a check, after avoiding it for six months. Or leaving the safety of your home to go shopping with a neighbor. The freedom of stepping out is only the beginning of all sorts of new frontiers. This is why it's essential to reward yourself for taking the risks, so that you continuously reinforce the positive steps you've taken.

At this stage look ahead, while at the same time recalling the principles that helped you to overcome the fear response. Life is never entirely free from fear, since anxiety is part of living and can be a response to the everyday stress we feel. If you're recovering from an illness, or had a major upheaval in your life, such as a separation, death of someone close to you, or job change, then you'll be more likely to experience a recurrence of fear symptoms. Just remember that we all regress temporarily, and so what! When we were children we didn't worry about wanting our favorite bear during a thunderstorm, even though we hadn't required it when the sun was shining. Sometimes fears and phobias can be a little like an old pair of shoes that are worn and not really needed, yet when our psyches are frazzled we tend to slip them on anyway (even though our new shoes are more attractive and far better for us).

At this point it's essential to look at all you've accomplished by overcoming your fears and phobias, whether by driving to visit a friend, taking a plane flight of forty-five minutes, or standing in an elevator that's going only to the next floor. At each step along the way you need to assess how well you're doing and congratulate yourself on trying. If most people felt one-quarter of the fear that you've experienced, many people wouldn't have left their beds, never mind doing what you've risked and accomplished! It's time to acknowledge and appreciate how hard the struggle was. I feel proud to have accompanied you on this journey and hope you will now become more vocal about your understanding that fears and phobias are real handicaps that are treatable. This is the way we make public a problem that is too often misunderstood by many people, including many professionals. By voicing your cure you can begin to help others in a similar way that you've helped yourself. It's important for all of us to join hands and support ourselves and each other in the human struggle to do something despite our worst fears. I do hope this is only the beginning of your journey and that your skills and talents will open more possibilities for you in every aspect of your life. As you expand your horizons, the fear response will be part of your history. Remember that the journey of a thousand miles begins with the first steps. Bon voyage!

NOTES

Chapter 1 Why Me?

1. Doreen Powell, "The Initial Contact with the Patient," in Robert DuPont, editor, *Phobias: A Comprehensive Summary of Modern Treatments* (New York: Brunner/Mazel, 1982), p. 28.

Chapter 4 The Inner Voices of Fear

1. George Serban, *The Tyranny of Magical Thinking* (New York: E.P. Dutton, 1982), p. 23.
2. Ibid., p. 27.
3. Ibid., p. 65.
4. Ibid.
5. Ibid., p. 66.

Chapter 8 Agoraphobia: The Fear of the Feelings

1. American Psychiatric Association, *Diagnostic and Statistical Manual of Mental Disorders III* (Washington: APA, 1980), p. 230.

Chapter 10 Do I Need to Explore the Unconscious Meanings of My Symptoms?

1. Bella H. Selan, "Phobias, Death, and Depression," in DuPont, *Phobias*, p. 134.
2. DuPont, *Phobias*, p. xv.
3. Sigmund Freud, *A General Introduction to Psychoanalysis* (New York: Permabooks, 1958), p. 327.
4. Manuel D. Zane, "A Method to Study and Conceptualize Change in Phobic Behavior," in DuPont, *Phobias*, p. 25.

Chapter 12   Soothing Yourself

1. "Relaxation Gains as Health Factor," *The New York Times*, 13 May 1986, p. C11.
2. Ibid.
3. Mark Teich and Giselle Dodeles, "Mind Control: How to Get It, How to Use It, How to Keep It," *OMNI* 10, no. 1 (October 1987): p. 54.

Chapter 13   Rewriting the Old Script

1. Teich and Dodeles, "Mind Control," p. 56.
2. Ibid., p. 54.
3. Ibid., p. 55.

Chapter 14   Nutrition and Anxiety

1. "Food and Brain . . . Psychiatrists Explore Use of Nutrients in Treating Disorders," *The New York Times*, 1 March 1988, p. C10.
2. Jane Brody, *Jane Brody's Nutrition Book* (New York: W.W. Norton, 1981), p. 242.
3. E. Orent-Keiles and L. F. Hallman, "The Breakfast Meal in Relation to Blood Sugar Values," *United States Department of Agriculture Circular*, no. 827 (1949).
4. Alan Goldstein, in M. Bricklin, editor, *The Practical Encyclopedia of Natural Healing* (Erasmus, Pa.: Rodale Press, 1983), p. 426.

Chapter 15   Exercising to Exorcise Your
Symptoms

1. Claire Weeks, *Hope and Help for Your Nerves* (New York: Bantam, 1978), p. 51.
2. Ronald Ley, "Agoraphobia, the Panic Attack, and the Hyperventilation Syndrome," *Behavior Research and Therapy* 32, no. 1 (1985): pp. 79–81.

Chapter 18   Recurrence: Just Another Challenge

1. Claire Weeks, *Peace from Nervous Suffering* (New York: Bantam, 1978), p. 181.
2. Weeks, *Hope and Help for Your Nerves*, p. 71.

INDEX

Self-Help Guides
from St. Martin's Paperbacks

HOW TO SAVE YOUR TROUBLED MARRIAGE
Cristy Lane and Dr. Laura Ann Stevens
_____ 91360-5 $3.50 U.S.   _____ 91361-3 $4.50 Can.

THE WAY UP FROM DOWN
Priscilla Slagle, M.D.
_____ 91106-8 $4.50 U.S.   _____ 91107-6 $5.50 Can.

IN SEARCH OF MYSELF AND OTHER CHILDREN
Eda Le Shan
_____ 91272-2 $3.50 U.S.   _____ 91273-0 $4.50 Can.

LOOK BEFORE YOU LOVE
Melissa Sands
_____ 90672-2 $3.95 U.S.   _____ 90673-0 $4.95 Can.

SELF-ESTEEM
Mathew McKay and Patrick Fanning
_____ 90443-6 $4.95 U.S.   _____ 90444-4 $5.95 Can.

Publishers Book and Audio Mailing Service
P.O. Box 120159, Staten Island, NY 10312-0004

Please send me the book(s) I have checked above. I am enclosing
$ _____ (please add $1.25 for the first book, and $.25 for each
additional book to cover postage and handling. Send check or
money order only—no CODs.)

Name _____

Address _____

City _____ State/Zip _____

Please allow six weeks for delivery. Prices subject to change
without notice.

TACKLE LIFE'S PROBLEMS

With Help From St. Martin's Paperbacks!